Praise for

LAURIE NOTARO

WITHDRAWN BY
WILLIAMSBURG REGIONAL LIBRARY

"[Notaro's] quirky humor, which she's previously show-cased in her cult-classic essays on girly dorkdom, runs rampant."　　　　*—BUST,* on *There's a (Slight) Chance I Might Be Going to Hell*

"Notaro is a natural comic, a graduate of the Jennifer Weiner school of self-deprecation, but she's best when she's being nasty."　　　　*—Houston Chronicle,* on *There's a (Slight) Chance I Might Be Going to Hell*

"Notaro is everywoman. She is every woman who has ever made a bad judgment, overindulged (you pick the vice), been on a fad diet, been misunderstood at work, been at odds with her mother or been frustrated with her grand-mother's obsession with Lifetime TV, while somehow being a little too familiar with the conflicted, star-crossed personages of those movies."

　　— San Antonio Express-News, on *I Love Everybody*

"Notaro's humor is self-deprecating, gorily specific, and raunchy."　　　　*—A.V. Club (The Onion),* on *Autobiography of a Fat Bride*

"[Notaro] may be the funniest writer in this solar system."
　　—The Miami Herald, on *Autobiography of a Fat Bride*

ALSO BY LAURIE NOTARO

There's a (Slight) Chance I Might Be Going to Hell

An Idiot Girl's Christmas

We Thought You Would Be Prettier

I Love Everybody (and Other Atrocious Lies)

Autobiography of a Fat Bride

The Idiot Girls' Action-Adventure Club

THE IDIOT GIRL
and the
FLAMING TANTRUM
OF DEATH

THE IDIOT GIRL
and the
FLAMING TANTRUM
OF DEATH

· · ·

Reflections on
Revenge,
Germophobia,
and
Laser Hair Removal

LAURIE NOTARO

WILLIAMSBURG REGIONAL LIBRARY
7770 CROAKER ROAD
WILLIAMSBURG, VIRGINIA 23188

VILLARD
NEW YORK

AUG = 2010

This is a work of nonfiction.
Some names and identifying details have been changed.

2009 Villard Books Trade Paperback Edition

Copyright © 2008 by Laurie Notaro

All rights reserved.

Published in the United States by Villard Books,
an imprint of The Random House Publishing Group,
a division of Random House, Inc., New York.

VILLARD and "V" CIRCLED DESIGN
are registered trademarks of Random House, Inc.

Originally published in hardcover in the United States by Villard Books,
an imprint of The Random House Publishing Group, a division
of Random House, Inc., in 2008.

Library of Congress Cataloging-in-Publication Data
Notaro, Laurie.
The idiot girl and the flaming tantrum of death: reflections on revenge,
germophobia, and laser hair removal / Laurie Notaro.
        p.   cm.
ISBN 978-0-8129-7574-1
1. Notaro, Laurie.   2. Humorists, American—20th century—
Biography.   3. Young women—Humor.   I. Title.
PS3614.O785Z4675   2008
814'.6—dc22   2008005250

Printed in the United States of America

www.villard.com

2 4 6 8 9 7 5 3 1

First Edition

Book design by Nancy Beth Field

To Nana

CONTENTS

THE IDIOT GIRL
and the
FLAMING TANTRUM
OF DEATH

The Lodgers

It could not have sounded more divine.

Tall, shadowy pine trees; a bubbling creek with clear, pure water; meadow upon meadow of swaying wildflowers; temperature in the seventies, and a cute little log cabin with a loft at a lodge.

When my husband suggested we get away for the weekend and celebrate my birthday in the White Mountains, I couldn't have been more enthusiastic.

To Arizonans, the White Mountains are an incredible escape a mere four hours' drive away; to the rest of the world, they're the place where logger Travis Walton said he got sucked up by a UFO and then disappeared for five days while aliens put things in places unseemly. To me, they were a place with no phones, no television sets, no computers, no fax machines, just a cabin with a wood-burning stove, a feather bed, and a forty-degree drop in temperature, which I especially needed since I had just received a zipper burn on the back of my neck from my dress by engaging in the mortally dangerous activity of going to get the mail while it was still sunny outside.

When I told my mother about my birthday plans, she simply said, "Must be a popular place. Your sister is heading up there, too, but at least her boyfriend sprang for a fancy hotel. Why won't your husband pay for a hotel? Why are you staying in an old shack with a woodstove? How can that be fun? I bet you'll leave with a nice case of lice."

"We're not staying in a shack. It's a cabin with a feather bed and a loft," I said, thinking that she was one to talk. I've spent a great deal of time and effort in therapy trying to forget the majority of my family summer vacations. They were spent driving roughly far enough into the desert and away from our house that we couldn't physically run back to it after it was discovered that my parents had only sprung for one hotel room for the five of us and it was 117 degrees outside, making escape far too sweaty an option. To make matters even more closely resemble the comfort level of Guantanamo Bay, my mother consistently struck a claim for one of the double beds as we entered the room by throwing her purse on it, digging out her bottle of Tylenol and her pack of Winstons, and then sprawling out with her eyes closed and her hand over her head. This not only left the rest of the family one bed for cramped quarters but created an undeniable bounty of opportunity for pinching, slapping, and pushing between my sisters and me and sometimes even my dad, to which my mother would respond by roaring from her yacht of a bed two feet away, "SHUT UP all of you! If you people haven't noticed, I'm on VACATION!"

We were additionally blessed as a slight, cool drizzle fell like mist as soon as we drove into the lodge driveway and then checked in. As I opened the door to the White Mountains cabin, it was exactly as I had pictured it—well, outside of the shag rug and the black fur of mold in the shower. My husband sighed peacefully, put his hands on his hips, and looked around.

"A whole weekend of this!" he commented excitedly. "Can you even believe it? Listen. I don't hear a thing but that slight prattle of rain hitting the tin roof."

"Wow," I said, smiling wide. "To think, four hours ago, the seat belt left a burn so extensive we could have added a side of A.1. and called it dinner."

I unzipped my bags and unpacked my array of snack options, then stood gazing out the window at the steady, patient dribble of rain. My husband spread out on the couch and cracked open a book. "This is the life," he said with a smile before he started to read.

"Wow," I said, still staring out the window. "You gotta love this rain."

"Yep," my husband said without looking up from his book.

"Love the rain," I added. "Oh, I do, I do. I dooooo."

I walked around the cabin, rolled around on the feather bed, and when I was done, it was still raining.

"What time is it?" I asked.

"Two-thirty," my husband answered, and returned to his book.

"Hmmmm," I pondered aloud. "Are you hungry?"

"You just ate a pack of Twinkies, four bags of chocolate Twizzlers, and twenty-two servings of Funyuns on the way up here," he said, not looking at me. "I got full just by watching you."

I walked around the cabin again, checked for stains on the sheets, and to see if the people before us had left any foreign hairs in the bathroom, because even though my own bathroom may be filthy as a truck stop, I at least know the filth is mine and from where it has emanated. Strange, unknown filth is another story altogether, and I am saddened to report that an errant hair—belonging to neither my husband nor myself—made a rather obnoxious appearance at the bottom of a hot tub in our hotel room and absolutely ruined our wedding night. My new husband, however, was not grossed out enough to refrain from pointing the video camera at it and pressing the record button, leading to an odd and uncomfortable situation later when my family viewed our honeymoon tape, thus forcing my mother to drag me into the kitchen to say, "That in there is a little sick. It's not too late. The pope will understand. You can still walk away."

After not finding any hobo hairs in the shower, I climbed up to the loft and looked at the rain from the window up there.

"What time is it?" I called from the loft.

"Two thirty-two," my husband answered with a sigh.

"Are you hungry yet?" I asked.

"Let's play a game," my husband suggested. "We could play 'I'll Give You a Dollar for Every Hour That You Don't Speak a Word.'"

"Hmmm, that's odd," I said. "Across the way at the lodge, a person on the third floor just looked directly at me and then shut their curtains really fast, like in a huff!"

"Why are you spying on people, Mrs. Kravitz?" he replied. "Please come down from there before we find out that the person you're spying on is a sniper."

"I'm not spying," I insisted. "I'm just . . . soaking in my surroundings. I'm taking in the scenery, and discovering who our fellow lodgers are."

"You know, this is how Hitchcock movies start," he warned me. "And then before you know it, I'll be the one running through a cornfield being stalked by a crop duster because my wife had to spend her birthday peeking in other people's windows."

"I saw something in the window and I looked as an automatic reflex. *You know that I am curious by nature*," I said. "If it was a pubic hair, *you'd* be the one taking pictures of it by now."

"And you were the one who said, 'Don't worry, my parents will think it's funny,'" he responded. "Now they look at me like I showed them a movie of what happened in that hot tub before we even got there."

"Oh, shut up, they totally thought it was funny," I said as I climbed down the ladder from the loft. "I'm going to take a walk around the pond, see what I can see."

"You mean spy," my spouse said.

"I mean *see*," I iterated. "There's a little lake next to the lodge, I'm just going to go down and poke around."

"All right, fine, I'll come with you," he said, putting his book down. "I don't want to get a knock on the door in an hour telling me that you've lodged yourself in a dumbwaiter or gotten stuck in a tree trying to get a better view inside of someone's room, Harriet the Spy."

As we left the cabin, I noticed a sweet scene near the lake as a young mother lifted her rather new infant up out of the stroller and faced the baby toward the water. "Look at that new mom showing her baby the ducks and the ducklings!" I exclaimed. "How cute. Isn't that cute?"

"It's all adorable," my husband said as he put his arm around me tenderly.

"Did you just see that?" I gasped as I pointed to the third-floor window of the lodge. "The curtain in that window whipped closed the second I looked up there!"

"I will give you *two* dollars for every ten minutes you don't peek into someone else's room," my husband said. "Or dessert! I'll buy dessert!"

"Oh, well, that will be nice," I replied. "Fat Girl Eats Gargantuan Chocolate Cake Alone While Husband Looks On in Silence and Other Diners Think to Themselves, 'Poor Husband with the Fat Wife. Why Can't He Stop Her? She's Just Getting Fatter.'"

This issue, in itself, has been a thorn in our marriage, because although I married a truly, really, super-nice guy, he has a defect. An unforgivable, loathsome, irritating defect. To me, it's horrifying and at times nearly repulsive, but I'm just being honest here by admitting that my husband is not a Dessert Guy.

I know. Even though it finally put me at ease by blowing a hole in my theory that he might be gay (listen—if you've played beard as many times as I have, both knowingly and unknowingly, you'll find yourself looking at even your dad with doubtful eyes), there's something about a man who would carelessly abandon his wife when it came to her favorite course. There's something about a man who can simply too easily declare himself a traitor when the waiter finally brings "the little menu," begging off because he's "too full," "would rather have another beer," or is "not really in the mood." I mean, I just want to scream, flick him on the head with the back end of a spoon, and inform him in a quiet, yet strong (hissing) voice, "Let's really think about this. When's the last time I asked you to do something for *your* benefit?"

If there's anything sadder than a chunky woman scarfing

down a dessert all by her lonesome, it's a fat girl with no boobs, but eating cake by yourself in public is pretty damn sad. Dessert should always be a group activity; it is *that* happy of an event that everyone needs to partake, lest those with the least self-control feel a little intimidated by the one in the group with an offensive 13 percent body-fat number (which I view as tragic, anyway; should we be shipwrecked together and find ourselves on a barren island, my body can survive for years off the stockpile in my ass alone plus an additional season for each upper arm, but Miss 13 Percent, sadly, will be dead by sundown). If a bite of chocolate mousse is so entirely offensive to select group members, let this be known: I'm not asking you to eat as much as me, I'm just asking you to *engage*. You can pretend, for all I care, take only one bite, it leaves more for me, anyway, but GODDAMN IT, don't make me eat dessert alone at this stage in the game; it's the least you can do for your fellow man.

"You'll buy dessert," I said carefully, laying wide the trap, "but I hate eating it alone."

"I'm not a Dessert Guy," my husband shot back strongly.

"I think I need a closer look at the lodge."

. . .

An hour later, in the lodge dining room as my bananas Foster was being set ablaze by our waiter, I was clapping gleefully in wild anticipation as my husband held a fork aimed at the flaming plate of joy and love as I had instructed—well, almost.

"This is the part where we clap!" I growled to him under my smile, still keeping the beat.

Just as we were about to dig in, I heard an odd noise.

TINK-thud-thud. TINK-thud-thud.

When I turned around to see what the noise was, I saw a man in his late thirties, early forties, with messy hair, talking to the hostess.

"Are you selling food?" he asked her.

"Do you mean to ask if we're open?" the hostess responded, looking a little confused.

The man stood there, looking at her for a long, long, long time.

"Uh, uh, um, yeah," he finally said.

TINK-thud-thud. TINK-thud-thud, I heard again, and this time it was getting louder.

"Yes, we're open," the hostess assured him, to which he nodded and vanished.

TINK-thud-thud.

"What is that noise?" I turned back to ask my husband, and that's when I noticed that my dessert fire was totally out and I had missed most of the bananas Foster pregame show.

My husband shook his head and chewed on a rum-soaked banana. "This is good," he said.

"I told you," I said with a giggle as I dug my fork in. "Look at what you've been missing all of these years when you just sat there and watched me eat like I was a zoo animal."

TINK-thud-thud.

"What is that?" I asked him again, and that's when I saw his eyes widen.

And the sound got louder, and louder, and louder until it was directly behind me.

TINK-thud-thud. TINK-thud-thud.

Out of the corner of my eye, as I pretended to be exception-
ally perplexed by the shape of a banana, I saw the cause of the
commotion: a woman who had the body shape of a pretzel nugget
passing by our table, moving with the ease of an iceberg. In each
effort of mobility, she raised her flabby, enormous arm with all
of her collective energy, lifting her metal cane, which had somehow lost its rubber-stopper-sound-muffler end, then ramming it
heartily into the floor, after which she would clomp her huge feet.

TINK-thud-thud.

From the corner of my other eye, I saw my husband swoop in
with a spoon and suck up a large percentage of the melted ice
cream and the gooey, ooey, rich caramel.

"Don't get carried away," I cautioned. "From now on you can
poke at it with your fork and maybe move stuff around, but the
rest of it is mine."

After the woman had passed, a hulking presence behind me
blocked out most of the available light, and it took every ounce of
self-control I had not to turn around to see if I was about to be
eaten by Lord Voldemort. Slowly, the figure passed by our table
like a storm cloud, and I saw it was the man with the messy hair
who had asked the hostess if she was selling food. He had the
biggest boobs I had ever seen on a man, big enough to not only
benefit from restraints but require brake lights. His T-shirt,
which had perky little capped lady sleeves, stretched brazenly
across his boisterous bosoms at the same level of stress that had
caused the hem to hover over his belt, exposing just enough belly
to make witnesses cringe at the impropriety and check their own
waistband. Bringing up his rear was a pear-shaped gentleman,
very heavy in the derrière, with graying temples, who appeared to

be the patriarch of the group. One additional man, who also looked to be in his late thirties, completed the group, and his outstanding physical characteristic was that one eye was sunk about a half inch lower than the other, and his skin emitted a pallid, waxy glow, almost as if he had freshly woken from a feverish bout of malaria. His spine slumped forward and a wet stain, roughly the size of a diseased liver, marked his shirt, stretching from his shoulder almost to his midsection.

The entire restaurant fell quiet with a hush that was solid and impenetrable as the family shuffled around their table and took their seats. There was no discussion, no small talk; they were every bit as mute as their fellow diners. All eyes were on them, drinking in their oddity, their lopsided eyes, their stains, and, of course, the mammary glands.

Slowly, as the group opened their menus to see what type of food was for sale, a murmur began to fill the restaurant back up again with the necessary noise.

"It's a family or a gang," I informed my husband in the smallest whisper, which I intentionally laced with intrigue. "Only crime or genetics can bind those kind of characters together."

"Family," my husband volleyed immediately. "I couldn't even imagine how many prison populations you'd have to cull to produce that sort of show. And no neck tattoos, dead giveaway. Plus, if it was a gang, who do think is the brains of the operation over there?"

I looked back over at the table and saw that all of them had an equally hollow look in their eyes, although they were all looking in different directions—out the window, at the front of the menu, at a fork—and their jaws hung wide open, as if they were buckets tipped at an angle.

"Do families like that really go on vacation?" I asked, finding it hard to believe. "I thought they just stayed home, added more newspapers to the already-six-foot-high stack, and watched their cats breed."

Then I wondered what my own family would have been like on vacation if none of us had ever moved away from home, and I imagined it would be at some casino hotel with a good view of downtown Phoenix. Around the dinner table at the all-you-can-eat chicken fingers and meat loaf buffet would be my father, who no longer spoke because of his seventeen stress-induced strokes, and myself and my two sisters as the three of us pinched, slapped, and threw garnishes at each other while my mother remained back in the room, sprawled out on one of the two double beds with her hand over her head, enjoying the morphine stomach pump she'd paid a doctor from Tijuana to implant.

Not a pretty picture, either.

"But what if they're holed up here in a cabin after pulling a job?" I asked my husband.

"A job?" he choked out. "Are you serious? Which one of them would you say isn't on disability? The man asked the hostess if she was selling food. I doubt if all of their brain cells pooled together are active enough to pull off the top of a Jell-O cup, let alone a heist."

"No, I'm telling you. Look at them over there, all lost in a whirlpool of criminal thought," I insisted as the man with the google eyes tried to catch a reflection of himself on the back of his spoon. "Not all scallywags are deviant and smart. Just like in any group, there are bound to be the ones who took Beginning Larceny more than once, you know. They're the ones on the short prison bus."

"Are you that bored that you really need to fabricate some drama?" my husband asked. "Because if you are, I'll sit you down on the couch and turn on the TV for our next vacation. We're supposed to be relaxing, and taking it easy. But all you seem to be interested in doing is getting yourself all worked up about a family whose tempo is considerably slack and who you believe is the James gang. Well, they're not. They're just a bunch of people with potholed DNA looking for the cheapest thing on the menu, I promise."

"Maybe they're planning on robbing us," I added. "Maybe they're planning on robbing everyone here. This lodge is in the middle of nowhere. No one would hear a thing."

"Yes, we're at a cabin in the middle of nowhere," my husband reminded me as he took the last bite of my bananas Foster. "We're not on the Riviera, we're not in the Caribbean, we're not even in Phoenix. What is the most valuable thing people bring with them to a log cabin? An iPod and a bag of marshmallows. I doubt there's a safe behind the microwave at the front desk with Vanderbilt jewels in it, and if someone wants our bag of marshmallows, I know I'm not the one willing to wrestle them to the ground for it."

"Listen," I hissed. "All I know is that someone has been peeping at me through windows, and so far, the Clan of the Cave Bear over there are my best candidates."

"Are you done with dessert?" my husband asked curtly as he took his napkin from his lap and placed it on the table. "'Cause I'd like to get out of here before you start putting people under citizen's arrest for having lopsided eyes and giant man boobs."

"I bet it's a disguise," I mumbled under my breath as I followed him out. "I bet they're faking being a special-needs family."

For the rest of the night, while my husband sat on the porch with his iPod earphones inserted in both ears, I couldn't stop thinking about that family. The facts fit, in my opinion; none of it added up. Why would they take a vacation all the way out here? They didn't look like the outdoors type. It wasn't like they were going to go hiking or skiing with their walking aids and huge butts. And there were no phones at the lodge, no televisions, no radio. What could they be doing all day? Over dinner they hadn't said one word to each other as far as I could tell, so conversation was out of the question. They didn't look particularly happy, or like they were on vacation. And, if the oldest "son" had to ask the hostess if she was "selling" food as opposed to "Are you open?" they clearly didn't get too much social interaction. I had only one feasible explanation for the whole scenario.

Bandits.

Then, as I was peeking out the window, I saw the group of them emerge from the lodge restaurant and head over to the biggest cabin on the property. I knew how much our cabin had cost, and it was an arm and a leg for a double bed with polyester sheets, a pellet stove, and dirty bathroom. Their cabin was a two-story deal with picture windows all along the back that looked out right over the lake.

"For a quick getaway!" I whispered to myself.

I jumped when I heard a noise behind me, and I saw our front door open.

"What if there's a machine gun in that cane?" I asked my husband when he stepped back into the cabin and pulled an earphone out. "The rubber stopper was off of it, and there could easily be a trigger in that handle."

"One more word and I'm putting this back in," he said, nodding to the earphone. "You're being ridiculous."

"What could they be doing over there? They have the big, huge, expensive cabin, you know," I added. "What *are* they doing over there? They didn't even talk to one another."

"That's how you know they're a family," my husband insisted. "Hand me the marshmallows so when they come to conquer us I can throw them our riches to avoid getting mowed down by a piece of medical equipment."

Then he gave me a dirty look, put his earphone back in, and went outside.

From across the way, I saw the clan mammary male lumber toward the front window, give me a long, solid stare like a Bigfoot, then reach over and shut the curtains.

• • •

The next morning, as we walked into the lodge restaurant for breakfast, I saw that my suspects were already there, slurping down oatmeal, crunching—open-mouthed—on toast, and allowing fluorescent-colored egg yolk to dribble down their chins.

Ah, what masters you are! I thought to myself in a teeny voice. Masters of deception! But I know your secret! At least I am fairly, roughly 50 to maybe 30 percent confident that I know your secret! I am 25 percent sure I know your secret. Even though if it really came down to it, I probably wouldn't bet money on it, to be truthful. But I am still keeping an eye on you!

"Right this way," the hostess said as she led us to the table right next to the clan.

Before I could squeal with glee over the endless spying possibilities, my husband cleared his throat and then said to the hostess, "I'm sorry, the light over here is a little bright for my eyes. Do you mind if we took that table?"

And then he pointed clear across the restaurant to an area that was completely empty and entirely out of earshot of my subjects.

"Sure." The girl shrugged, then led us over to the darker part of the establishment and pulled out a chair for me.

"Oh, no. No, no," my husband piped up. "My wife will be sitting in this chair. With her back facing the rest of the restaurant."

I shot him a dirty look, sat in the bad chair, and took the menu the hostess offered me.

"This is so unfair," I hissed after the hostess had left.

"Shhh!" my husband demanded. "We're going to have a nice meal, and if the only way we can do that is by severing the use of your senses by blocking your access, then so be it."

"But—" I tried.

"No buts," he said firmly. "Not another word about it or you'll be eating breakfast dessert all by yourself. Understood, Valerie Plame?"

"After your performance of 'Watch Me Eat the Entire Bananas Foster in Three Bites' last night, I'm not so sure that's such a punishment," I shot back. "I'd rather share custody of children that weren't yours than go through that again!"

To my dismay, however, the family finished their grub, got up, and left before we even got our food. I watched them through the window as they plodded across the drive of the lodge and to their log cabin. As the alpha waddled to their car and opened the trunk, I ascertained that he had had the hugest ass I'd seen on any man. I took another bite, closed my eyes for a moment in pure joy, and when I opened them again, the man was draped in black straps hanging from both shoulders.

As I looked closer, my mouth fell open almost wide enough to allow French toast to fall out.

They were binoculars. Four pairs of binoculars, two swinging from each side, in addition to several camera cases. And, in front of him, held by both of his hands, was a rather large telescope.

"Holy shit," I whispered as I watched the father look all around to him to see if anyone was watching, then head right back toward the estate cabin.

"What now?" my husband said with a sigh as he put down his fork and looked at me tiredly.

"'What now?'" I mocked him as I pointed out the window. "*What now?* What now is that I just saw the fat-assed dad take a whole bunch of surveillance equipment from the trunk of his car into the house. That's *what*."

My husband turned around just in time to see the man step into the cabin and shut the door behind him.

"Wow," my husband said as he turned back around.

"I don't want to say I told you so," I admitted. "Because even I was doubting my theory up until about ten seconds ago."

"Well, hang on," the spoilsport replied. "Let's not get ahead of ourselves. Just because they have a rather large stash of stuff doesn't mean they're—"

"Spying on their fellow lodgers?" I interjected. "Looking to see what everybody's got in their cabins without having to pose any risk of getting caught? Well, guess what? If they're planning to spy on me, I'm going to beat them to the punch. No one's getting my marshmallows! God! I need some Tylenol!"

I took six more very quick bites of my French toast, asked the waitress to charge the meal to our cabin, and stood up.

"What are you doing?" my husband asked, looking panicked.

"I'm going to go and see what *they're* doing," I explained as I folded my napkin and placed it on the table next to my plate. "You can come with me, or you can stay here. Either way, you need to leave the tip."

My husband shook his head, stood up, and followed me outside.

"What are you going to do?" he asked as I marched out into the sunlight toward the lake, taking the same path I had the day before.

"I'm not going to do anything," I said as I waited for him to catch up. "I'm just going to walk past the back of their palatial cabin and see what's going on behind those massive picture windows."

Just then, my husband gasped. "Don't turn around," he warned. "But someone was just looking at us from a window up at the lodge and closed the curtains as soon as I saw them."

"What is this, a stakeout? Do they have a lookout up there?" I cried as I got closer to the lake. "Are we surrounded on all sides?"

"Wait, wait," my husband said, grabbing my arm just as the back view of the estate cabin came into sight. "Wait. What are you going to do if they *are* peeking into people's cabins with binoculars? What are you going to do?"

I stopped. Honestly, I hadn't thought of that. At all. I suppose it was a good question—just what was I planning on doing? Was I going to yell at them to stop it, inform the lodge, or call the police and tip them off that people at the lodge I was staying at had binoculars . . . and were *using* them? I would get the same kind of response I got when I called the police on the county fair, thinking it was a party down the street and that someone was playing a Loverboy album awfully loud. "It *is* Loverboy. They're working for the weekend," the officer who answered the phone said, then uttered a guffaw and delivered a dial tone.

"I don't know," I said truthfully. "I was pretty much making this whole thing up before I saw all of their Peeping Tom equipment. I have no idea what I'm going to do."

"Well," my husband said, then paused. "Maybe you should start by looking up at the second floor of the cabin right now."

I turned around, and there, all gathered on the terrace of the second floor, was the entire family, all four members of the freak show. The ample-bottomed father was setting up the telescope, the mother already had her face stuffed into a pair of massive binoculars, and the man with googly eyes was slurping on a grape Popsicle as a purple stain spread down the front of his shirt. The man with Tara Reid–esque boobs was flipping though a small book, and when he looked up and saw us, he smiled and waved.

I waved back. Their binoculars and telescope were facing out, toward the lake, not in, toward the cabins.

"Bird-watchers," I whispered.

"You're an asshole," my husband whispered back.

I turned around and started walking back as quickly as I could.

"Where are you going?" my husband shouted after me.

"I'm going to try and get back to the restaurant before they clear our table," I announced. "I still had six to eight good bites of that French toast left!"

But as I got closer to the main lodge, I saw the third-story peeper out in front of the lodge next to a truck, and the peeper saw me. There was no doubt about it. She looked to her left and then looked to the right, then finally realized I had gotten a good look at her and gave up all hope of a smooth escape.

"What are you doing here and why are you spying on me?" I asked the peeper point-blank when I got about two feet away; I was very, very tempted to reach out and deliver an open-handed slap. Right across the thigh, where I knew it would hurt the most.

"I hate family vacations," she said. "I didn't want you to feel like you were on one."

"Well, I can't see Phoenix, can you?" I replied. "Mom said you were staying in a fancy-pants hotel."

"I have a hotel room at the lodge, and you have a cabin at the lodge," my sister explained. "Why would I tell her I was staying at a lodge? She'd tell me that the sheets would be dirty and bugs would get into my hair and then lay eggs. I saw you yesterday when you guys pulled in and I've been holed up here, trying not to run into you or make you feel obligated. I got out of the dining room this morning just in time. Boy, you should see the cast of characters we sat next to. There was a man with boobs like a strip-

per and a man with eyes that rolled around in his head like
Cookie Monster's."

"Tell me about it," I said, shaking my head. "Do you have any
Tylenol?"

"Are you kidding? I'm on vacation," my sister said, looking in-
credulous. "Of course I do. I was just thinking I could use some
myself."

Stink Bomb

I wish my husband would stop getting the newspaper, because now it all makes sense. Angelina Jolie is a line of cocaine and I'm just a burp born after a sausage sandwich. I look like what a belch smells like, and all because men are basically nothing but bald monkeys.

No, I didn't accidentally take the same medication twice today. What I'm talking about is real science! Real science, people!

According to a story I just read, researchers at Massachusetts Institute of Technology's Sloan School of Management have published results that indicate "seeing a beautiful woman triggers a pleasure response in a man's brain similar to what a hungry person gets from eating or an addict gets from a fix."

So, see, Angelina is a big heaping pinkie nail of blow, and the rest of us are the brownish liquid that gathers at the bottom of the crisper when the organic vegetables you bought in the spring at the farmer's market repeatedly lose out to the ease of a box of the Jolly Green Giant. When men see Angie, they just want to inhale her, but when the opposite sex spies me coming, all they want to do is light a match.

The scientists went on to say that "feminine beauty affects a man's brain at a very primal level, not on some higher, more intellectual plane," like that's some sort of news flash. Us women have known that for years, but really, it's probably not any man's fault. After all, how intellectual can they get when their brain is working at the same level as the coordinates of their fly?

Still, the news is rather disappointing; even though it came as no surprise to me that I would never reach supermodel or, apparently, heroin status. You see, it's hard for a girl to give up hope—there's always the possibility that Neutrogena will come out with a pore-shrinker rinse or that Clinique will invent a foundation that gives you perfect, plastic skin you just peel off at the end of the day. But with this latest revelation, walking around completely aware that I am a stink bomb in physical form is almost enough to make me be nice to my husband, because by now he's simply used to the smell, and I should be happy that he's not trying to fumigate me with Oust every day.

The trouble with this story is that things your mom taught you to make you feel better about being ugly were never even mentioned. It's not like the scientists said, "Well, at first glance, men equated Laurie with a large head of simmering cabbage, yet, because of her kindness to strangers and her great personality, they upgraded her to a plate of Brussels sprouts swimming in a delightful butter sauce." There's simply no option for an upgrade like "a great sense of humor" or "oh, she's just so great with kids" because either you're pretty or you're not. End of story. And that's double bad news, because I don't possess any of the upgradeable attributes after all.

Then I tried to debunk the whole study by pointing out to my husband that no one ever even heard of the stupid school the study was conducted at anyway, until he pointed out the *M*, the *I*, and the *T* in the initials.

And then commented that it was obvious that *someone* in the room most likely had eaten a sandwich of spiced meats and looked straight at me.

Death of a Catchphrase

Last Saturday night, at approximately 8:23 P.M., the phrase It's All Good quietly passed away while appearing in a prime-time commercial for Buick. The cause of death was officially determined as "overexposure," though the phrase had indeed lived an extended and prosperous life, having a long-standing returning role on *The Jerry Springer Show* and *The View*.

Survived by his wife, You Go Girl!, and his children, Don't Go There and Talk to the Hand!, the slang star was born in a school yard when several third-graders were fighting over a piece of Laffy Taffy and it fell onto the ground. Kenny Moses, a grammatically challenged fat child, scraped the dirt off of the taffy with a Popsicle stick and proclaimed, "It's All Good!" After spreading through the school like wildfire, it was apparent that the phrase showed promise of a future in slang when several adults repeatedly asked, "Will you please stop saying that! What does that mean?" Soon It's All Good found a home in the hallways of middle and high schools. It was just a matter of time before someone noticed that It's All Good had star quality with a potential for greatness.

Spotted soon after in a nightclub by agent and retired slang star Dy-NO-mite!, It's All Good immediately signed with the once household name and found himself trudging to cattle calls.

"It was hard on him," said Dy-NO-mite!. "You go to these auditions, you give them all you got. You're spit and polished. And for what? They come back and say, 'Sorry, we need something with more pizzazz,' or 'Thanks, but we're really looking for a noun.' That gets to you, man, that can really eat you up. There were a couple of auditions when I thought, 'This is it!' but later we'd find out that it went to *Hasta La Vista, Baby,* or *Run, Forrest, Run!* Those were hard times, I tell you, hard times."

Finally, however, It's All Good got his first big break into slang when he played a brief and nearly unnoticeable part on an episode of *The Fresh Prince of Bel-Air.* Star Will Smith decided to use him at the last minute, replacing No Way, José, who had just checked into drug rehab for the third time. Within weeks, It's All Good was appearing on every episode and soon became a regular, which led to guest spots on *Dawson's Creek, Felicity,* and *Dharma & Greg.*

"All of a sudden, It's All Good was everywhere," remembered his wife, You Go Girl!, who met her future husband on the set of *Ricki Lake.* "It was overnight, it seemed. People couldn't get enough. He was on the tip of everyone's tongue."

His star was riding high. Jay Leno, Letterman, and Conan were calling. There was talk of an HBO special, a record deal, and an opening slot on the Britney Spears tour, and rumors were flying like gunfire about a possible Budweiser campaign. Things were looking great. And then disaster struck.

Negotiations with the beer giant crumbled when It's All Good insisted that his younger brother, It's All Aight (commonly known simply as Aight), be included in the campaign as well. Worried that "Aight's" troubled past and affiliation with Sean Combs (then known as P. Diddy) would negatively affect the campaign, Budweiser pulled its offer when It's All Good refused to budge. Word got around that he was difficult to deal with, and the phone stopped ringing.

"He got a fat head," Dy-NO-mite! recalled. "But then another brother team, Wasssup? and What Are YOU Doing?, was hired for the campaign. That was the nail in the coffin, man. Punks!"

It's All Good dropped out of sight, and it seemed that his once brilliant career was over. Younger, more splashier slang expressions such as No You Di'in't and All Ate Up started to fill his spots, and most people, with the exception of teenage, truck-driving males in Yuma, Arizona, and Mudlick, Idaho, began to forget their former favorite expression.

Despite the production of bumper stickers, T-shirts, and Post-it notes with his image, It's All Good was on his way to has-been status. But one day last fall, it looked as if his luck was about to change. Dy-NO-Mite! received a call from Buick, which was looking to create a "trendy and dope" ad campaign. And they wanted It's All Good for their slogan.

"I found him in a seedy slang bar, sitting in between Keep On Truckin' and Where's the Beef?," the agent recalled. "It was pitiful. He had begun selling some of his letters, even vowels, to pay for the booze. I almost didn't recognize him. 's All Goo, 's All Goo,' is what he said to me. He was a broken phrase, just broken."

His agent cleaned and sobered him up and took him to the shoot. According to people on the set, the talent of It's All Good had not faded, and he produced what some say was his best work to date. It was a glorious comeback. Tragically, however, it wasn't to last.

When the first Buick commercial aired on Saturday, It's All Good uttered his last breath and quietly faded away to the other side.

"He'll live in our hearts forever," You Go Girl! said as she wiped away a tear, "or at least on that Buick commercial until next year's models come out. I heard No Way, José got that part."

Sickening

When I found my seat on the airplane, the woman sitting beside me looked completely normal. She wasn't missing teeth, she didn't have any pronounced facial scabs, her hair appeared freshly washed, and I sincerely doubted that the octogenarian sitting next to her was a deputy extraditing a passenger. So, when she open-mouthed coughed as she was flipping through the airline magazine, I politely cleared my throat. When the second open-mouthed cough shot out of her like a bullet approximately a minute later, I cleared my throat again and gave her a warning look, which involves furrowing my brow, turning the corners of my mouth downward, and deeply expressing with my eyes "If you want to keep coughing like that, we'll give you a sedative, put you in a crate, and stick you in the cargo hold with the rest of the live-stock." After approximately sixty seconds had passed and she erupted her foul lung discharge with no preventative barrier yet again, all bets were off and I reached into my purse and pulled out my bird-flu mask.

Curiously enough, the next cough that came from her body was, as expected, blocked by her manicured hand, which had finally roused enough initiative to reach up and cover her rictus of a mouth. Apparently, nothing says "Pardon me, but I've seen better manners on African dictators who use skulls for candlesticks. Kindly resist the compelling urge to spread your foul disease via your cannon of a mouth by simply covering it" like an N95-rated bird-flu mask that barely leaves anything but my eyes visible and lets everyone on the plane know that I drew the short straw and got the seat assignment next to Typhoid Mary.

To be perfectly honest, I wasn't always the kind of person who keeps a bird-flu mask in her purse just in case she finds herself in an episode of "When Open-Mouthed Coughers Attack." Nope. I used to be the kind of person who would ignore the vestiges of illness and was even known on occasion to extend an acknowledgment of blessing should someone sneeze in my company. But no more. Once you have seen the white light of disease, there is no going back, there is no ignoring the things you have been enlightened about. And for me, it happened on a sunny Saturday morning when I was flipping channels while enjoying a hot cup of tea, unaware that what I was about to see would bring to my life change in such epic proportions that I would begin to carry nothing short of a hazmat suit with me at all times. On that Saturday morning, I began watching a Discovery Health Channel show about how people get sick.

And there, on the television, was Holly, a girl who was standing in an elevator with a man who was getting ready to destroy her life.

He coughed on her.

Poor Holly. There she was, completely unaware while millions of minute mucus particles, each carrying the flu virus, exploded into the air like rain. It was their germ mission to land on her and try to find their way into an opening of her body, much like a date I once had attempted with me. Then one successful particle invaded her through her nose.

It was all over.

I knew how Holly felt, because I had been sick three times that fall, and I wasn't about to let it happen again. In fact, I suspected that my most recent illness was due to a lady who had gotten into an elevator I was in and coughed all over me like she was plucked out of the Middle Ages before she got off on the next floor. Now that I had seen Holly's show and knew how germs worked, I was going to protect myself.

My husband, however, saw danger.

"What is all this?" he asked when he came home as I was unloading the groceries I had just bought. "Antibacterial hand wash, antibacterial tissues . . . do I sense an obsession?"

"No," I said simply. "It's not an obsession. It's not an interest. It is my new way of life. I am now a germophobe."

"Why can't you have another hobby?" my husband pleaded. "Like exercise or dusting? Laundry would be a *very* good hobby for you. Think of how healthy we could be if we actually had clean clothes! Oh God. You watched a Discovery Health Channel show about cold and flu germs, didn't you?"

"I will just admit to being more aware of the bacterial challenges around me in the everyday world than I was last night when I went to sleep," I confessed.

"I thought we agreed that you weren't going to watch 'Things That Invade Your Body' shows on Discovery Health Channel anymore after what happened last time," my husband said with a very stern face.

He, of course, was referring to the parasites and tapeworm documentary we watched together about people who had gone to crazy, unsanitary places in the world and had come back with some new friends in tow, such as jungle butt worms. My husband was particularly horrified by the story of one gentleman who had recently returned from Vietnam with a new pal he named George, which was a worm that lived—kindly steady yourself— under his skin and would travel all over his host's body, until one night while he was on a business trip and staying in a hotel, the host spotted George wiggling across his upper thigh, had enough, grabbed the closest sharp object, which I believe was a ballpoint pen, and dug that little asshole out. While my husband writhed in disgust, I promptly added Vietnam to my list of Places Too Gross, Too Lacking in Private Potties, or with Entirely Too Vague of a Cuisine to Visit (any country that considers the heads of animals as dinner gets on the list).

That, however, was nothing, I felt, compared with the story of a massage therapist who had just returned from some other parasite-ridden landscape and was giving a massage to a client when she suddenly felt something "cold" in her panties. Curious, she excused herself and went to the bathroom, and when she pulled down her pants—pardon me, my gag reflex is threatening to resurface the gyros I just ate for dinner—deep breath. Deep breath. Deeeeeep breath. Kittens are so cute, aren't they? God, kittens are cute. So cute! And puppies. I love puppies. They should have a cute-off, kittens and puppies. I really don't know who would win, to be honest, puppy breath or a kitten chasing a fly? Um, okay, back down the hatch. I'm just going to have to write this very fast—when she pulled down her pants, a worm flipped out and landed on the floor. A worm. A WORM. I, myself, taking a cue from the Unabomber, would have tried to hang myself with those panties AT ONCE and WITHOUT DELAY, because I'm sorry, having knowledge like that is no way to live. I was born in Brooklyn, New York, for a reason, and that reason is that New York has a very good water-filtration system, which enables its population to rest easy knowing that worms won't launch out of their panties when they go to the bathroom.

Now, it is true that I had a dream in which I was in Africa, sitting outside a tent, and it was very hot when I looked down and I saw something pink and folded just sort of heaped there, and I thought to myself, Is that . . . ? Nah. Couldn't be. Could it? Oh my God, it is. It is. Goddamn it, my vagina just fell out! And I didn't know what to do, because how do you stick something like that back in? A vagina isn't a Lego, it doesn't just snap back into place with a playful push and a *click*! But it was just lying there in the dirt like a little pink wind sock. I knew it would be bad to have a dirty vagina, so I picked it up off the ground with a stick, then approached a man in a white coat, presumably a doctor, to see if he could put it back in. But when I tapped him on the shoulder, he, unfortunately, turned out to be Noah Wyle, and then I was just too embarrassed to ask him to help me return my genitals to their rightful place, so I put my pink wind sock in my purse with the intent of finding someone significantly less attractive to give me a hand with it later. It's true, I had that dream, and honestly, it is a struggle for me to look in the mirror every day knowing that in some imaginary realm, my cookie fell into the dirt like a pork chop breaded in filth and hay particles. I have to deal with that. But apparently, this massage therapist was not raised a Catholic like myself but most likely in a much looser, "Sunday-only" religion like Protestantism, because she pulled her pants up, picked that worm off the ground, stuck it in her pocket to show it to her doctor later, and went right back to work without being bound by even the thinnest thread of shame.

Now, I only *watched* that show, and every time I felt the smallest little tingle, tickle, or hair moving on any part of my body, I would have to stop from tossing myself into a bleach vat or in front of a flamethrower, convinced that I had a colony of Georges tearing across my scalp in a worm race or that I had a tapeworm the size of a reticulated python trying to sneak out my back door. For weeks after, my diet streamlined down to foodstuffs that could not be found in nature, such as Oreos, Diet Coke, Funyuns, and anything else that supported a parasite-hostile environment and consisted solely of chemicals and cancer-causing agents. In the bathroom, I could barely touch the waistband of my underwear without having a full-blown "flippy worm" panic attack. And then, when I was finally beginning to forget about the butt worms and Georges of this world, my husband and I were at dinner at one of our favorite restaurants—a wonderful ramen place around the corner—when I took too big a mouthful, attempted to bite off the noodles I couldn't accommodate, and while almost all of them splashed back into the bowl, one curly, white stray ramen noodle fell onto the table, at which my husband pointed his fork and then said simply, "Did you wanna put that in your pocket?"

So it is easy to understand how all of the sympathies I once had for that man have evaporated, and how utterly simple it was for me to completely ignore him when he vocalized his concern for my newfound fear of germs and viruses. If he couldn't take the lurking danger seriously, then I had to focus on myself. I was concentrating on germs. From now on, I decided, shaking hands with people was out of the question. Instead, I would just say "Nice to meet you" and then wave at them energetically or blow them a kiss. There was no way I would touch a public door. The surface of a doorknob holds a lottery of sickness, not to mention bits from people's bodies. I used a paper-towel shield or pushed the door open with my rear end, since that area is usually protected by a very firm and impenetrable butt shaper, and germs seeking refuge down there would simply bounce off of the industrial-quality Lycra.

Touch a handrail on an escalator? You've got to be kidding! Those things are nothing more than conveyor belts of pestilence and filth, serving up a buffet of maladies and horror that would rival any petri dish in the labs at the Centers for Disease Control. Grab on to one of those things and you're toying with unleashing the Apocalypse. Then we have shopping carts equipped with handles acting as flu and cold lightning rods, and don't forget about airplanes, which recirculate air, creating a fan that spews out a wind tunnel of various afflictions. And if I ever heard someone cough, I'd sprint the other way like an Olympic athlete on some very good drug that her coach told her was flaxseed oil.

But it was on a plane ride to Eugene, Oregon, after spending Christmas in Phoenix, that I really became a true and devoted convert to germophobia. Now that I live in a small town, the planes I take reflect that small-town John Cougar Mellencamp size and are basically Fisher-Price toys with car engines controlled from the ground by a baggage handler with a joystick.

We all crammed on, all of us Fat Christmas People on a tiny plane, and that was when the symphony began. The coughing. The sneezing. The sniffling. It didn't help matters that we were leaving Arizona, the state that was currently having the worst flu outbreak in the country—so bad it was a top story on CNN's headline news. Now, I know people have to travel home whether they're sick or well, and I can't argue with that. But what I do take issue with is when the breathing cadaver in the seat behind me coughs and coughs and coughs hard enough that I feel his lung g-force hit my head and it makes MY HAIR MOVE. That cough had the wind-tunnel action of a Dyson and was easily strong enough to push-start us down the runway. And it was grotesquely apparent from the unmuffled sounds that the coughs had been released with reckless abandon—there had clearly been no obstacle to their discharge into the world. The man behind me was an open-mouthed cougher. No hand action to shield the rest of us from the germ cloud rushing from deep within his lungs—not even a Kleenex to provide a thin, flimsy barrier.

To make matters worse, he wasn't the only one; the plane was full of them. And I don't get this; I mean, really, where are these people when Dr. Gupta says it again and again on every news show, "To help prevent the spread of disease, wash your hands, cover your mouth, and stop blowing your nose on your Tommy Bahama shirt"? Do they not get the Discovery Health Channel? Did they not know of Holly's plight? Who are these open-mouthed coughers? In which dark corner of society do they live? These people, I assume, must be these the same ones who leave pee on toilet seats and let gum simply fall out of their mouths onto the sidewalk. Being sick is not like e-mail—you don't need to spread it around to a hundred people to have the gods shine on you or get better. Keep your death rattle at home, I say, because I don't want it. In fact, I think making people stay at home when they're contagious should become a national policy. Sickness has the same properties as people who look at porn on the Internet. Keep it where it belongs, in private. No one wants to know your secret, and no one wants a visual.

For some people, however, that might not even be enough. For repeat offenders, for all of those selfish people who continually cough and sneeze on others when they're sick, I believe we need a quarantine unit set up. If you simply can't manage to raise your hand six inches to cover your gaping cavern of illness, go ahead and skip that step. But the next time you commit that offense it will be in a whole roomful of renegade nose-blowers and other open-mouthed coughers just like you who can infect each other repeatedly instead of contaminating the healthy population. If you sneeze once or twice, well, that happens, but more than that, it's the sickroom for you. And when you're quarantined, you're *quarantined.* There will be a special sick restroom, complete with receptacles in which to dispose of your snot rags properly, like a bonfire, and yes, there will be excessive pee on the seats. And, so the sick can eat, there will be a sick vending machine, outfitted with already contaminated buttons.

And it was during that flight from Phoenix back to Eugene that I made myself a promise: I would never, ever, let myself be that exposed in a such a turbulent atmosphere again without recourse, showered continuously with microscopic particles of infection just searching for a new orifice to invade and set up shop.

I spent the rest of that flight with my napkin acting as my sad interpretation of a SARS mask, covering my nostrils as best it could from the germ shower being shot at the back of my head, and when I got home, I did the only thing I could do: I went online and bought two cartons of bird-flu masks. And then, several days later, I came down with a cold that quickly turned into pneumonia and made my lungs crackle like a bag of Tostitos being danced on every time I took a breath.

And with the memories of the Christmas flight and the two weeks I spent in bed crackling, I did not feel one bit bad, weird, or overreactive as I looked at the woman sitting next to me as she open-mouthed coughed on me one last time, then reached into my purse and prepared to snap that bird-flu mask over my head. Not one bit.

But before I could get the mask securely over my face, I was hit with something silent but deadly and oh so potent, heavily spiced with yesterday's broccoli and sauerkraut, something that I was sure came shooting from the octogenarian sitting next to Typhoid Mary, rising up in a toxic attempt to smother and kill us all.

Oh God, I thought as I held my breath. Someone help me. I've seen *that* Discovery Health Channel show, too.

Love Thy Neighbor

If the envelope had been delivered to the wrong address, I would have torn into it with glee. But it's never a happy event to get a letter from the police department delivered to the right address.

Yours.

Standing next to the mailbox off my front porch in the middle of summer, I held the envelope in my hands and wondered as a wave of dread washed over me. No one ever gets a nice, happy letter from the police department unless it begins with the words "Good news! The charges against you have been dropped!"

And then I breathed a sigh of relief.

How stupid am I? I laughed. Duh. I knew exactly what the letter was, because I had gotten several of them before. It had to be a notice that I was being fined because the alarm on my security system had gone off without reason. Much like the last time I was charged $150 because the alarm had sounded when a thief tried to kick in my back door, failed because of the dead bolt, ran away when the alarm went off, and was gone before the police got there three hours later. In the rule book of the Phoenix Police

Department, apparently, if the hoodlum fails to gain access to your home and flees the scene but leaves a calling card of a split doorjamb, a footprint on both your back door and the door to your storage shed, you owe the city of Phoenix a nice little non-deductible donation/early Christmas gift. In the time it took the police to respond to the alarm that someone was breaking in to my house AND WAS BREAKING IN NOW, the thief could have entered my house, surprised me on the potty, tackled me as I tried to shuffle to safety but fell because of the pants around my ankles, hit me over the head with the Bigfoot mug my husband gave me for my birthday, then skinned me like big game with the paring knife in my Henckels set (which he was going to steal any-way), wore my skin like a dress around the house, watched *Death to Smoochy* on DVD, and farted into my couch cushions before he realized how boring my house was and left because it turned out that the $2.84 in coins he found scattered all over the hallway floor from my pants pockets was actually sufficient to buy a value combo meal and a shake at Jack in the Box.

And, just after he left, that would be the moment when the police show up and make a note to fine me $150 for a false alarm.

Great, I thought with a heavy sigh as I tore into the envelope; I didn't even know I had been almost robbed again. I unfolded the letter and then gasped like I had just seen a parent naked.

"COMMUNITY NOTIFICATION," the letter announced in bold, all-capital letters, then went on to inform me that a notifica-tion must be made when certain sex offenders are released from Arizona State Prison and that one of them had recently moved into the neighborhood.

Well, I said to myself as I tried to diminish my fear in any way possible. Surely, this guy, Kenny Ray Swain, whose picture was presented in grainy black and white, showing his devil-like eye-brows, his beady, glaring, pigeony eyes, and his tight, wide lips that curled in a snarl like a sinister comma, didn't do anything too bad. Maybe he's just one of those guys who courted a seventeen-year-old in a trailer park and she fibbed about her age, right? It could be something like that. Or maybe he was just doing some heavy breathing into a phone receiver late at night, or maybe he was simply stealing panties from clotheslines and dryers in Laun-dromats. It could be something like that, right? Right? It proba-bly isn't anything serious at all; nothing like being convicted of one count of sexual assault, one count of sexual abuse, three counts of kidnapping, one count of unlawful imprisonment, and "other crimes." It couldn't be anything in which during the of-fense, Kenny Ray Swain forced his way into an apartment, beat three guys up so badly they couldn't help the woman who was also in the apartment, who Kenny Ray Swain then raped.

Kenny Ray Swain, it was clear, was not just a regular, ordinary, selling-porn-thru-the-mail or stealing-ladies'-undies brand of sex offender, but an Ed Gein variety of sex offender because in that one night of horror, Kenny Ray Swain was a lone wolf. He did all of that by himself, and was ranked at class three, which the aster-isk placed along side of his title noted was a "high risk to the com-munity."

Well, no shit.

In addition, the letter read, "Citizen abuse of this information to threaten, intimidate, or harass sex offenders will not be toler-ated."

I already had my head between my knees and was fumbling

for my inhaler when I looked at the letter again and realized that I hadn't even seen the most important part, which was listed at the bottom. Kenny Ray Swain's current address was on the same street as my house was. His house number was 1201. Mine was 1218.

In fact, it was the brick house.

On the corner.

Three houses down from me.

I had to put the letter down. I couldn't read any more. If I picked up the letter again I was afraid it was going to say, "Turn around slowly. He's behind you and it's too bad you don't have three male friends over, because Kenny Ray is in the mood for a PARTY."

I didn't know what to do first—scream, pack my bags, or beg my doctor for testosterone shots to complete my canvas of dark, *Magnum P.I.* facial hair. I wasn't necessarily afraid to be in my house—after the would-be $150 false-alarm phantom burglar, we installed wrought-iron security doors on every entrance, adding to the wrought-iron security bars we had bolted to every window (completing our "It's a 'Hood Thing" theme) years ago after another burglar broke in while the house was being restored and before we moved in, stealing a radial arm saw, a stereo, and my bathroom sink, then pooping outside on the patio, leaving it alongside the shirt he took off and wiped his ass with. I would trade almost all of the insurance money I got just to see the look on his face when the urge hit him and he realized our bathroom not only didn't have a toilet but also was missing toilet paper and a floor.

One thing I knew I wasn't going to do was call my mother for comfort. "Oh, so there's a pervert living on your street, huh?" I was sure she'd say. "Well, in your neighborhood, big surprise, now there's that one plus the four you don't know about that have been watching you walk around in your bra for ten years. I'm telling you, every house with filthy windows has a pervert inside. Animals. Dirty minds have dirty windows. Everyone knows that. But I wouldn't worry about the Super Rapist if I were you, especially if he gets a good look at you from behind. I'd say you were probably pretty far down on his list."

As I looked at that letter in my hand, my fear rapidly gave way to unbridled anger. I was furious. Didn't we have enough to deal with on our street without adding a rapist to the soup? Come on, my inner whiner cried, we just got down to eleven remaining feral cats across the street; the family who liked to throw parties every weekend and knew a mariachi band, turning their backyard into a live *Sábado Gigante* set, finally moved away; and Auggie, our local Gang Activity and Event Coordinator, recently violated his parole and went back to the clink. Things were looking *up*! Why do *we* get the rapist? Can't another neighborhood take him, just to give us a break? I wonder if we can broker a deal with another neighborhood, I thought. Maybe the people over in Garfield would be willing to trade for him. I'd be willing to swap half a dozen hookers and a bum who pees in the open for Kenny Ray. And a meth lab. We could do a meth lab. Not a big one; I was talking kitchen sink/bathtub sort of operation, but yeah, I thought, nodding to myself, we could do a meth lab. I'd be willing to trade for that.

Because one little rapist, no matter how tiny, can ruin a whole neighborhood, and I mean *the whole thing*. Their damage is concentrated, and it can go a long way, like anthrax or Ann Coulter. I just didn't get it. How did he end up on my street? How did he end up three houses away from me, just like that? How did he move in without anybody knowing anything until this letter arrived? How did someone help him move a rapist's couch into his new rapist living room without immediately running into the street and yelling, "Hey, everybody, you might want to stock up on some pepper spray and whistles, because you've got a live one here!"

I wondered if I had passed him on the street, stood in back of him in line at Safeway, or sat at the table next to his as we both ate chile rellenos at Tacos de Juarez. How would I even know? It wasn't like he was extending the courtesy of wearing a T-shirt that said YOUR NEIGHBORHOOD SEX OFFENDER on it or even a little rubber bracelet with CLASS THREE AND ROAMING FREE embossed on it.

The thing that got me the most is that it just wasn't fair. It wasn't right that one man could make hundreds, if not thousands, of people live in absolute terror and not have been elected into public office by popular vote. Why can't he go live with his own kind, I wanted to know, in a gated trailer park community with all of the other rapists and classes of predators and deviants, where they can finally know what it's like to live with one of their own among them, where they're the ones afraid to take the trash out at night or even walk a dog? Where the safety of their daily lives gets to be altered and threatened because a neighbor who counts kidnapping and sexual assault as hobbies. They could call it "Attack Acres" or "Offender Heights" or even "Asshole Land." I didn't care what they called it, but I wanted Kenny Ray Swain to move there; I wanted him to get off my street and let my neighborhood go back to being the nice little shithole it was before this letter landed in my mailbox.

. . .

When my husband came home that night, I didn't say anything, I just stood there and handed him the letter.

"What's this?" he asked, and he sighed. "Why am I looking at this? Oh no. Oooooohhhh no. If you have another pen pal that you've neglected to tell me about, the answer is no, he can't crash here while he goes on work release doing the night shift at Waffle House. There are two perfectly good halfway houses within a two-block radius of here that would be happy to have him and those crazy Charlie Manson eyes. And that's final."

"Oh, it's too late for that, my friend," I cried as I shook the letter at him. "It's too late to ask for permission. He's already here. Look at the address. And why I told you that I tried to lend my comfort and support to a lonely, grammatically challenged soldier in Desert Storm who failed to reply after I told him I wore bike shorts under skirts is a mistake I will never make again, and it does not mean I will lick a stamp for just anybody! I was writing to a patriot, not a convict, although it's not my fault that both commonly misunderstand the function and nature of preventative undergarments."

"Oh my God," my husband said with a gasp, reading further. "He beat three men into unconsciousness? Alone? What is this, Crouching Tiger, Hidden Rapist? Does he fly and run across treetops? How long are his nails? What do you think his record for man beating is? Do we need four guys in the house at all times?

Do we need five? You know, I could start a band and we could practice here."

"Yeah, I'd feel really safe knowing that there were five guys in grandpa sweaters and horn-rimmed glasses arguing about whether it's 'nah-nah-*nah*' or 'nah-nah-*neh*' in my living room, just waiting to beat a rapist with a programmable drum machine and a sound-effect pedal," I replied. "You could use a guitar as a weapon, but which one of your friends with their pasty Grover arms would be strong enough to swing it? What I'm most pissed about is how the city raised our property taxes because we finally replaced the broken front window, but no one felt the need to let us know that the Night Stalker would be in the area until he's moved in and is getting his prison mail forwarded to a house I can see from the same window."

"This is an outrage," my husband declared, balling the letter up in his hand and shaking it. "I am outraged."

"There's nothing we can do about it," I complained. "It's not like we can walk over there and tell him to move on, because we're not allowed to harass him; citizen abuse will not be tolerated. There is no committee we can go to. We are entirely powerless here. We can live in fear of him, but don't even think about saying anything to him. How do you even approach a convicted rapist? 'Hi, my name is Laurie, I live three houses down. Please don't defile me'? My God, I need to pamper myself right now. I want a Milky Way Midnight bar, some raspberry sorbet, and six rolls of Charmin Ultra Soft. I'm going to the store."

"Wait!" my husband said as he grabbed my arm. "You can't go to the store alone. I can't let you go out there by yourself. It's too dangerous now."

I felt the blood rush to my ears as I got even angrier. Where was I, Saudi Arabia? Kenny Ray Swain moves onto my street and now I can't leave the house without a male escort? Ever? I can't *ever* go outside? I wanted nothing more than to march over there and pepper spray him just because, even if it was 110 degrees out, which made it even more like Saudi Arabia.

And then suddenly, it hit me, much as if Kenny Ray were to sneak up behind me and clobber me with something big and dull and skull-shattering. It was 110 degrees out. At night. Who was I kidding with all of this "going outside" business? I hated going outside. I loathed going to the store, fighting traffic, and dealing with the crush of humanity that existed just beyond the other side of my front door. Hadn't one of my all-time favorite reveries been to become a cranky hermit, live unperturbed in my house, and have things brought to me like a monarch or tribal lord? At the very least until the end of the summer, because, really, if Auggie, who was merely a gang cruise director, couldn't control himself without screwing up and returning to his maximum-security gated community, what were the honest chances of a class-three felon on the same street not breaking his parole and going straight back to making tattoos with a shard of glass and a ball-point pen on the bottom bunk before fall came?

Now you might just say to yourself, Oh, look, isn't that cute and optimistic, God gave Laurie a lemon and now she's making lemonade, but the truth of the matter is that God didn't give me a lemon, he planted the Lex Luthor of all rapists three frigging houses away from me, and figuring out just how to survive now in my house wasn't exactly mixing a pitcher of Country Time. It was more like chewing on the lemon rind and then attempting to

swallow it under the threat of a whirling dervish of a deviant predator who could come calling for his obligatory cup of sugar at any
moment. This, coupled with the fact that the only times I have
lamented not having children are on days it was too hot to go out
and get the mail, run to Sunshine Mart to pick up a candy bar, or
fetch myself a refreshingly cold beverage without having to leave
the comfort range of the oscillating fan, forced me to arrive at a
very rancorous, yet delightful, conclusion. Kenny Ray Swain, for
the time being, actually solved some long-standing issues.

"This is so unfair," I whined, stomping my foot. "All I wanted
was a Milky Way and some sorbet. This has been a horrible,
frightening day, and I just wanted a moment to forget it all. And
now I can't even go out! I might as well throw on a burqua. My
life as I know it is over."

"Don't worry," my husband said, lifting the car keys from
his pocket. "A Milky Way Midnight? Raspberry sorbet? And
Charmin, is that what you said?"

"The extra-soft Charmin," I replied, slowly and sadly nodding.
"Blue package. The pink package is so rough it's like planks of
wood. The Dairy Queen in Apache Junction has softer toilet
paper than that. Oh, no, and I forgot we're out of milk, too, and I
feel a pudding crisis coming on. And we're down to one egg,
which is not good, because I may need the solace and comfort of
French toast for dinner. Do you see how my whole life just fell
apart? My *whole life*, just because I'm a woman, and just because
of one selfish rapist! I can't even get myself an egg!"

"I'll take care of it," my husband assured me. "I'll be right
back. Don't answer the door. And here's the phone in case you
need to call the police, but I'll be back before the requisite three

hours it takes them to show up, so understand that 911 is just a formality, in case they slap us with another false-alarm fine. Are we up-to-date on the life insurance policy?"

I nodded demurely, then watched as my husband left the house, made sure he'd locked the door, began sweating immediately, then proceeded to get into his barbecue of a car and kill thousands of his own brain cells as they boiled to death inside his skull like a pot of macaroni on a stove.

I, in turn, grabbed a Snapple, still wishing I had offspring or a nicely trained monkey to fetch it for me, plopped my hiney down into the cushions of the sofa with a *pop!* as I opened my diet raspberry iced tea and made sure I was directly in the path of the fan.

Now, much to my amazement, my husband kept up his knight-in-shining-armor routine for a week and a half, maybe two, and I have to say I could not blame him when the errand-boy life got a little stale. I sent him out almost every single night, sometimes twice if I was especially thirsty and the only thing that could save my life was a cherry limeade from Sonic (with two cherries in it. *Two. I'm a prisoner in my own home, so I ask you, is two cherries one too many to ask?*), while I stretched out on the couch and made him do my bidding because he was the gender that Kenny Ray only beat into unconsciousness. It was devilry. I know it. But resisting was futile. It was kind of like having a butler, but one that you could wear pajamas in front of and pinch if he made you a little mad. I was a little resentful, however, when he stood by the window for the first time and mentioned blithely, "There goes the ice cream man, and it looks like he's having a sale on those cookie bars you like so much. Sure wish I had some shoes on . . . like you do," or pointed out that Maria Elena, artisan of the most exquisite tamales anywhere in the world and one of my main reasons for still living in that house, had hit up everyone on the block but us with her stolen grocery cart and five-gallon bucket.

"Maria Elena is walking around out there just fine, and he hasn't gotten *her* yet," my husband noted. "Maybe you could go out to the car and kind of . . . see what happens."

I got the hint completely and finally ventured back outside into the heat, but I felt much better when I had the "in case of fire, use to smash windows and attempt to bend the iron security bars until you peacefully succumb to smoke inhalation" crowbar in my hand that I kept beside my bed that had been left at our house by the burglar who used his Journey T-shirt for, I was sure, the rough kind of Charmin.

. . .

I guess I'll never really know if it was the crowbar, the quality of my posterior view, or the fact that maybe our neighborhood scared even Kenny Ray, but I never came into contact with my neighborhood rapist; in fact, I never saw him, not once. As far as I know, he never left his house. I never saw him in the front yard practicing pouncing or springing from bushes, but maybe he simply hated 110 degrees as much as I did. Or maybe he was just as terrified of showing his mug to the thousands of people who must have gotten that letter as we were afraid of seeing it.

Eventually, over the next several months, I began leaving the crowbar at home more often simply because I would forget it and things started to level out, little by little, almost to the point that most days I even sort of forgot I had a class-three sex offender, kidnapper, man attacker, and abuser living 150 feet away from me. I know this was mainly because I wanted things to return to normal more than they had reason to, but it was an easy con. It became something that hung in the background like the warnings on cigarette packages; the danger was always present, always there, and always a second away, but with each day that passed without us coughing up blood, the farther away that warning seemed and the less it had an impact on our lives. Every day, it drifted farther away, and eventually, the goldenrod-colored letter from the police department with Kenny Ray's thin-lipped mug shot on it became simply another piece of the puzzle on our refrigerator door, next to the pictures of our nieces and nephews, above and below recipes, coupons, and reminders. In a very odd way, we got used to living nearly next door to a violent, dangerous, but invisible rapist.

I don't know what happened to him, and for that matter, I don't know if he ever really lived there. I have a feeling that he did, because whoever lived there put a 1978 burlap sleeper sofa, a tree stump, and the obligatory broken dryer out in their front yard crowned by a FOR SALE sign, and four weeks later, the neighborhood pack of wild dogs had torn the stuffing out of the back of the sofa and peed all over the stump, the door to the dryer had fallen off, and the sign had changed to FREE, so my vote says "yes," although I can't prove it. But I still have that letter.

I did know, however, that the next time I got an envelope from the Phoenix Police Department with my address on it, I was going to jump for joy if it was a notification of a $150 fine for another false alarm.

Happy Birthday and the Element of Surprise

It wasn't my idea to go to the store.

It wasn't my idea to be standing in line with the cashier and everyone in the general vicinity scrutinizing me, but there I was. It had all begun fifteen minutes earlier when I had perched myself in front of the bathroom mirror, unable to move.

"My nose is getting bigger," I said aloud, studying it as closely as I possibly could.

"I'm going to unscrew the lightbulb in the bathroom if you don't come out of there soon," my husband said as he sat on the living room couch, trying to read a book.

"Did you hear what I said?" I complained louder. "I said my nose is getting bigger, and that's not all. So are the pores on it. One of them on the tip of my nose has gotten so large I swear I saw a hand come out. Apparently, a small child from Texas mistook it for a well and fell into it."

"Stop it," he insisted.

"I can't," I said as I shook my head. "I just found a trio of hairs that are trying to colonize one of my necks. If I don't stop them now, it's just a matter of time before their relatives from New Jersey arrive to homestead a nostril or plant sideburn crops."

"This is no way to spend your birthday," he said, finally putting the book down and getting up. "Come on. Let's go to the store, grab a nice bottle of wine, and sit out on the deck. It's seventy-five degrees outside and the sun will be setting in about an hour. Doesn't that sound nice?"

To be honest, anything sounded better than scouring my chest for a follicular Jamestown, and we still had several hours until our dinner reservation, so I made the better choice of catching a tiny little birthday buzz over scouring my body for age spots. To put it lightly, it was not an ordinary birthday, it was one of those Milestone Years in which you do not only investigate every visible inch of yourself (and would fully attempt, if possible, to search your own cavities to see how those areas were holding up as well), but go to the secret, bad place and open the Dusty Vault of Youth. That's where you keep the photos of yourself taken in the precipice of your vitality that you hold next to your current hag face to tally up how much damage has been incurred. It's also the place where you keep the last bra you owned that required no lowered tone when telling a Victoria's Secret salesperson the size, the last thing you owned that bore horizontal stripes, and an ashtray that you, while inebriated, pried out of a cab with a butter knife when it was still cute and "unpredictable" to do those sorts of things. Should I attempt that same act of taxi unpredictability at my current age, I'd be shot in the ass with a heavy dose of lithium by county health services and then either get dropped off by the train tracks or given a free bowl of soup and a bed at the

Mission if I agreed to let someone ramble some gospel at me from the good book. While the trauma of discovering three-inch-long stealth hairs that had been flourishing long enough that I could have knit a hat out of them was enough to push me to the brink of considering skin grafts from a Norwegian, I was in need of something *now*.

So *vino* it was.

"You know, the only benefit to being this old," I told my husband as we got into the car, "is that the likelihood of a barren psychopath mistaking my girth for a ripe pregnancy, following me home, forcing me inside at gunpoint, and slicing open my belly only to discover that the baby is actually a ham-and-cheese sandwich with a side of potato salad has just dropped dramatically."

"See?" my husband said as he backed out of the driveway. "Now, that's the kind of birthday spirit I wanna hear!"

At the grocery store, we picked out a decent wine and then presented it to the cashier, who looked at the bottle, then looked back at us. Then she cleared her throat and made history as the Person Who Took Bumper Sticker Wisdom Far Too Literally.

"I need to see your IDs," she said quietly, practicing a random act of kindness.

I choked on my own spit.

Now, true, since we live in a university town, I am sure the manager at Safeway insists that all of his cashiers are diligent about carding, but I suspected a different motivation altogether.

In my head, I assembled the options quickly:

a. She'd just taken her last hit of Ecstasy before her shift, sniffed some paint, or had a tooth pulled and is high on some top-quality pharmaceuticals.

b. She believes my husband to not be my partner for life but my underaged offspring.

c. She's a barren psychopath who is trying to determine if I'm still of childbearing age and if my paunch is an indication of a yawning fetus or simply decades of bad living and poor choices.

d. Bribing the cashier is my birthday present from my spouse and we're not going to dinner after all. And nothing makes me angrier than hunger.

But my husband, on the other hand, thought nothing of it, mainly because he doesn't hold a photo of himself at twenty up to his reflection every five years to assess road wear, and he can still fit into the pants he wore when we were dating, although he, too, keeps an old 34C bra of mine in his sock drawer to remind himself why he married a woman who now has black yarn growing out of her neck. He pulled his wallet from his pocket without a second thought and handed his driver's license over. The cashier nodded, handed it back, and looked at me.

I pointed to myself and raised my eyebrows. "Me, too?" I asked.

"Yep, you, too," the young woman, who looked to be slightly past the drinking age herself, said politely, and then I suddenly understood that this might be for real.

She might really want to see my ID, I think to myself as I feel a tingle dance up my spine. I might really be getting carded.

I might really be getting carded!

And all of a sudden, I realized I was glad. Happy. Thrilled. Flattered. Delighted. It was more than that, it was wonderful, and made me realize how foolish and masochistic I had been, holding up a picture taken in my twenties and chastising myself because I had aged a little since then! In that mirror at home, I had just hit an ugly Milestone Birthday and was decaying minute by minute, but in Safeway, I was possibly under twenty-one. UNDER TWENTY-ONE. Holy shit, I thought, the light in here must be great. I love Safeway light, I love it! I am never leaving. I am moving to Safeway. I felt my ass tighten, I felt my stomach get flat, I felt my pores shrink to the size of pudding cups. I was young again, and my birthday didn't matter. I'm not old, I said to myself. I am not middle-aged. I look like a Rolling Stones song. I rock. If you took a picture of me in the Safeway light, I bet it would have looked pretty darn close to the glamour shot in my Dusty Vault of Youth.

I felt *so good.*

So naturally, I couldn't leave it at that and enjoy it. Of course I had to poke at it until it burst.

As I handed over my driver's license, I humbly, almost bashfully, added, "Oh, I bet I'm old enough to be your mom!"

To which the cashier promptly noted as she handed my ID back to me, completely innocently and without malice, "Actually, my mom is younger than you are."

Instantly and without hesitation, my ass made a plopping sound as it hit the floor, the seams on my jeans popped like gunfire as my stomach returned to its regular size, the hair on my neck sprouted to a length that made Rapunzel's look butch, and my spine lurched forward as I suddenly lost 70 percent of my bone mass.

Apparently, the look on my face embodied all of these physical atrocities, and if that wasn't bad enough, I even saw my husband wince. It was not lost on the cashier, who quickly tried to remedy the situation before I needed the assistance of a Hoveround to leave the store.

"But my dad is older than you," she offered. "By a lot."

I smiled weakly and wrestled with the urge to reply, "Who the hell is your mother, Loretta Lynn?"

"It's all gooooood," she cooed at me as she handed my husband the receipt and we left the store.

"Boy," I said to my husband as we got into the car. "That was more fun than the birthday you took me to the pound to get a dog and pointed out which ones were going to be put down next."

The minute we returned home, I raced for the phone, picked it up, and dialed my best friend, Jamie, who lived in Marina del Rey, not only because she's my best friend but because her birthday was exactly one week earlier. If there was anyone who would understand, it was Jamie.

But it was Jamie's husband who answered the phone, and he had some news of his own. "Guess what I did this weekend," he said.

"Took your wife out for dinner for her birthday?" I asked.

"Oh no, better," he informed me. "I threw her a surprise birthday party!"

"*You did not!*" I said, gasping, completely unbelieving. As a man, he did simply not possess the skills of organizing a sandwich let alone something as complex as a social gathering with a purpose and that also involved advanced levels of trickery.

"I DID!" he boasted.

"You're lying!" I replied.

"I'm not," he insisted. "I really threw her a surprise party!"

"Were there other people there besides the two of you?" I questioned suspiciously.

"Yeah, like twenty," he replied.

"And they were there on purpose?" I asked. "People passing by or people you can see through a window and who might be able to see you back don't count, you know."

"No, no, they were invited," he said.

I was stumped. "Put her on the phone," I demanded.

"Hi!" my best friend said.

"He threw you a surprise birthday party?" I asked immediately.

"No," she said.

"He said he did," I informed her.

"Oh, I know," she answered. "He's very proud of himself."

"But you didn't get a surprise birthday party?" I said.

"No," she confirmed. "I did not."

"So you found out about it?" I asked.

"Oh God no," she said, gasping. "He kept that little nugget to himself."

"Do not spare one detail," I demanded.

Apparently, several days before the event, it came to her husband's attention that Jamie's birthday was exceedingly close, and like many men who go to Target in search of a gift for their wives but come out empty-handed aside from the Xbox they have purchased for themselves, he was at a loss.

And then he had a brilliant idea. Gazing at his Xbox and realizing how happy he had made himself, he remembered that it was his friend Oscar's birthday, too. Maybe Oscar would also get an

Xbox. Maybe they could have an Xbox war! And then he remembered that Oscar's wife, Maria, had sent out invitations to Oscar's
party for that very weekend.

For Oscar's *surprise* birthday party.

Jamie's husband made a phone call to Maria, and like any
nice, young wife trying to do something special for her husband's
birthday who was suddenly backed into a corner by his friend, she
agreed politely to make a trade.

Jamie's husband would buy the decorations, put them up, and
pay for half the cake if Maria would pick up the cake, then have
the party at her house as she had originally planned.

And it was all set.

Jamie and her husband arrived at the party, hid with everyone
else when Oscar was close to coming home, and shouted "SUR-
PRISE!!!!" when he finally walked through the door. They min-
gled with all of Oscar's friends, drank some wine, and Jamie's
husband pointed out the pretty decorations. Then it was time for
the cake.

As Maria brought out the cake dotted with tiny, festive candles, everyone began to sing the familiar song, "Happy Birthday
to you, happy birthday to you, happy birthday, dear Oscar . . ."

And then one little, tiny, but proud male voice rang out suddenly, "and Jamie!"

"Happy Birthday to you!"

Jamie, thinking her husband a bit of a jokester, most likely
grinned at his little insertion, but it wasn't until her husband
brought her over to the cake that she realized the magnitude of
what was happening.

"Because there, Laurie," my best friend recounted, "in all

fancy, big red letters, was 'HAPPY BIRTHDAY OSCAR!' on the top of the cake, and then on the bottom, in teeny-weeny, little tiny, last-minute 'Hey, could you stick this on there, too?' letters was 'and Jamie!'"

"Oh my God," I said.

"And that's when he turned to me and said, 'Surprise!'"

"When did you punch him out?" I wanted to know. "Because you'd better tell me you punched him out!"

Jamie wisely abstained, because at that moment, knocking her well-meaning husband to the ground took a backseat to what she saw displayed on the dining room table with candles sticking out of it. At first sight, Jamie believed it to be a mountain range covered in snow with a red rose topping each of the peaks, but as she continued to stare at the cake, she realized that what she believed to be Kilimanjaro was, in stark and triple-X reality, a gigantic pair of enormous cake boobies.

I gasped. "You mean to tell me that not only did he hijack another guy's birthday party," I said slowly, "but you got a titty cake for your birthday?"

"I got a titty cake. I guess the left and larger breast was Oscar's," Jamie told me. "And mine was the right one. I believe I ate an areola. *That* was surprising."

I started to laugh, and Jamie started to laugh, and soon I couldn't even make any sound at all except a clicking in the back of my throat that resembled dolphin talk. I even tinkled in my pants a little, but honestly, I was surprised that didn't happen without provocation when I was standing in line waiting to get my ID back.

Because as crappy as my birthday had been thus far, no mat-

ter how badly I thought it sucked, one thing was true: I highly
doubted that at the end of the night anyone, let alone a room full
of strangers, was going to see me put an areola, familiar or otherwise, into my mouth.

And that, certainly, was something to celebrate.

Leaving, but
Not on a Jet Plane

The first thing that popped into my head when I saw the
FOR SALE sign in my front yard was, What the hell is *that* doing
there?

I gasped and felt my head spin a bit. Don, our Realtor, must
have sent his guy over in the morning to put it up, I realized. I just
hadn't expected it so soon.

We were leaving.

We had known we were going for some time now, but up until
this point it had all been talk. Talk, talk, talk. I got the distinct im-
pression that no one believed us, and to be honest, we barely believed it ourselves.

Almost a year earlier, my husband had decided that he had
not run up a significant enough amount of student-loan debt, and
that if you're going to borrow money from the government, you
might as well borrow enough so that they put a lien against your
house, otherwise you're just going through the motions. He filled

out the applications to numerous graduate schools and sent them off, and we barely talked about it again until he got a big envelope in the mail six months later, read it, then looked up at me and said, "Hey, um, could we move to Chicago?"

"If you're getting extradited, I'll visit," I offered. "So sure, move to Chicago."

"I got into grad school," he said plainly.

I paused for a minute and tried to catch the little nugget he had just thrown at me. Did he just say he got into grad school? He got into grad school. Now, it wasn't like we had never known any grad students, or that I didn't think my husband had it in him, but he had applied to some good schools. Really good schools. Schools that were a little hard to get into.

"You got into *grad* school?" I asked, just to make sure that he hadn't said "bad school" or "sad school."

He nodded.

My head started spinning, and then it started spinning faster, and faster and faster. "You got into *grad school*?" I asked again, only this time a little more loudly, and a little more excited. "You got into *grad school*?"

"YES!" he said with a big smile.

His smile, however, was nowhere near as big as mine.

"Do you know what this means?" I asked, a second away from hopping up and down. "*Do you?*"

"I don't know, what?" my husband said, his eyes lighting up.

"I dated a retarded person, you know!" I laughed as exhilaration washed over me in big waves and my hands flailed. "Actually, I'm pretty sure I dated two, but I didn't mention one because he said he didn't have a driver's license and was only sort of illiterate, so I just count the one. And now you've gotten into grad school! Which is incredible! This is so fantastic! This is awesome! I'm so happy!"

The joy on my husband's face was diluted only slightly by confusion. "So . . . this means we're . . . moving to Chicago?"

"It means that by getting into grad school you canceled them out!" I said, now fully jumping up and down. "I can't believe it! I can't believe it! My record has been cleared! It's been restored! Atonement! I have achieved atonement! I never thought I'd live to see the day!"

"I will still never understand how you didn't know he—now they—weren't special-needs people," my husband said, shaking his head.

"His mouth was gripped around that bong 95 percent of the time," I answered. "How could anyone even tell the difference? Goofy grin, never a full sentence, always laughing. And they all watch cartoons. Trickier than you think, my friend."

"All right, all right," my husband said impatiently. "Back to grad school. And Chicago."

"Unless there's another Chicago fire, I doubt we could ever afford a house there," I said reluctantly, but I promised to look into the real estate market of the Windy City to see if there was anything we could swing.

And there was: I found a basement apartment in a section of the city that had the highest gun rate per capita and crime rates to match.

"I'm all for you being smart," I informed Mr. I Got In. "But we already live in Crack Village. I don't know how excited I am about downgrading from the 'hood to a ghetto, to be perfectly honest. I like my tweakers, rapists, and arsonists from the desert, a little dehydrated, weak, and experiencing mirages. They're easier to manage and distract with a bottle of Gatorade or the wave of a garden hose."

"I just really wanted to go to grad school," he replied with eyes so sad they belonged on a seventh-grade girl who didn't make first-round cuts for the pom squad.

"I don't want to die because you're not retarded," I explained softly.

Then a big envelope from Indiana came.

"We could buy the governor's house, and the governor's mother's house," I said. "But as soon as I uttered the words 'separation of church and state,' we'd be chased all the way to Chicago by people carrying torches and riding John Deere equipment."

Then another big envelope came, this one from Arizona State, from which my husband had just graduated.

"All right," he conceded. "I can go back to ASU, I got in there. At least I know where all of the best public bathrooms are on campus. At a new university, I'd have to scout them out all over again, and that could take years. I have a month to make up my mind, and if no one else accepts me, then I guess we have a plan."

I nodded. It sounded good to me. And he waited and waited. Checked the mail every day, called me at home if he was gone for the afternoon to see if the mail had brought another big envelope, and always, without fail, the answer was "no." No one else had accepted him, that was clear, so the day before ASU's deadline, he made an appointment to see an advisor to say that he'd accept their invitation for grad school.

And that's exactly where he was, walking up the steps of the

English department building, when Hugo, my mailman, came and delivered another big envelope.

From Oregon.

"Don't go in, don't go into his office," I said in a fit of panic when my husband answered his cell phone. "Oregon is here. Oregon sent you something big."

And with the sound of tearing paper, we were pretty sure we were moving to Eugene, Oregon.

I booked two plane tickets to the small college town, and we made the trip up, not exactly knowing what we would find. And really, I didn't even know what to look for. I hadn't moved since 1972, when my parents decided that Brooklyn was a crappy place to raise three little girls and hauled us to the desert of the then quiet and unassuming town of Phoenix. I didn't even go away to college. I didn't know what to look for when scouting a potential homeland. So after three days of driving around in our rental car through the streets of Eugene, we found ourselves back at the tiny airport that had one security metal detector and a plug-in digital alarm clock that sat on the floor. The guy who checked me in at the ticket counter ran past me on the escalator and was the same one to take the ticket back before I got on the plane.

"It's a small place," my husband said to me as we waited for takeoff, which involved, I was sure, the ticket giver/taker running at full speed toward the small jet and then push-starting it until the engine turned over.

"It's really green here," I replied.

"There isn't a gray cloud of pollution sitting on the city like a hat," he added. "I can't believe how many stars we saw last night."

"When we passed that community garden, I swear I could smell the onions," I offered.

"I'm pretty sure that was the BO wafting from the stinky hippie who was checking his pot plants," he informed me. "You should have lived here in your twenties. You could have dated a different retarded boy every night."

"Trees line every street," I realized aloud. "It's like a movie set. I think I might like it here."

"Are you sure you can do this?" my husband asked. "It's a big thing."

"My body hasn't emitted a single drop of unsolicited perspiration in three days, and in the same amount of time, we drove around and never got flipped off once," I concluded. "There's no decision to be made."

• • •

Over the next couple of months, I hired electricians, carpenters, roofers, painters, and plumbers to finish up every project I had started during the eight years we had lived in the house so it would be perfect when we put it on the market. I figured out which days the nearby Starbucks and Einstein Bagels got their deliveries and fished their perfect-sized boxes out of the dumpster in the blistering heat of summer. Every week, I packed ten of those boxes and sent them with my husband to the storage unit we had rented. We had it down to a science.

We were really moving.

I couldn't wait to get out of the heat. That last summer was the worst one I could remember. Things like taking a simple trip up to Safeway required monumental proportions of stamina, a will to live, and at least one bottle of water, lest you got stuck at a red light during the four-block ride. You've never wanted to get out and literally rip the skin off the head of someone so bad as you did the asshole in front of you who stopped on the yellow. People say it's a dry heat, like that erases the fact that it's entirely within the realm of possibilities of desert life that a body can become mummified without even dying first and if you go on a lunchtime hike in the middle of the city and only bring one bottle of water, you'll be coming back down that mountain in a metal basket at the end of a rope attached to a medivac helicopter. I myself was once teetering on the precipice of spending eternity as a grimacing, angry piece of limbed leather before I spotted a Sonic and the treasure of cherry limeade just in the nick of time. I now have a yellow, desiccated pinkie with an excessively long fingernail as a result of my jeopardy, but I live to tell the tale. You don't understand 114 degrees, day in and day out, until you live in it and feel the life being roasted out of you, droplet by droplet. To me, walking outside in July, even at 7 A.M., is like getting slapped in the face with the hot hand of my mother the first time she caught me smoking one of her cigarettes.

Once all of the projects were completed in the house and I had filled up the storage unit with things my husband said I didn't need but I decided to keep out of spite, I set out to conquer the biggest project of all: Creating the Ultimate Fantasy. Now, for some people, the Ultimate Fantasy might consist of water-balloon boobs on a faux blonde who has a mouth that opens but never says anything, or a diamond ring so big it can fry ants with a glint of its reflection, but for me, the Ultimate Fantasy meant something altogether different. It came to life in a thirty-six-dollar bottle of olive oil packaged in a stoneware crock with an olive tree, a scroll, and an address in France printed in dark green and was sealed with a bubble of red wax I spotted on a shelf in Williams-Sonoma.

And in an eighteen-dollar aluminum-and-pine box of gourmet salt tied with rustic twine; in a large, squat glass jar of strawberry-rhubarb preserves; and in a French blue-and-yellow canister of crêpe mix that bore a delightful flat pancake wearing a beret and a devilish little red neckerchief on the label.

I went home with a Williams-Sonoma bag filled with Ultimate Fantasy components and systematically threw away every box of anything that could have been bought at Safeway and was visible, including Aunt Jemima pancake mix, Bertolli olive oil, Welch's grape jelly, and Morton's iodized salt.

Peasant food.

The people who live here, I told myself, do not ingest grape jelly on toast. They politely spread strawberry-rhubarb preserves on their croissants in the morning as they read *The New York Times* and admire the sunflowers fresh from the farmer's market that sit in an antique pitcher in the middle of a table dressed with a crisp, white linen tablecloth. They do not read mass-market paperbacks with dog-eared puffy covers and Junior Mints melted over the spine; rather they enjoy hardback works of literature, both classic and modern. Needless to say, my husband was delighted to house his collection of Emily Dickinson, Mina Loy, Herman Melville, and Edna St. Vincent Millay in the bookcases that flanked the fireplace as if they were all illegitimate children he was finally encouraged to acknowledge.

And so it was.

It did not matter that the person who really lived there often ate frosting from the can with her finger as an after-dinner treat, owned *Death to Smoochy* on DVD, or had once fought a fire in her backyard, set by (a) a vagrant, (b) a Crip or Blood, (c) a prostitute, or (d) an itchy-fingered tweaker, in her underwear with a garden hose at three o'clock in the morning. Or that she wore that pair of underwear for so long it was returned to its primal state as a loincloth, with an inch of fabric attached to the waistband in the front and another piece in the back, and she found it one day, garishly displayed on her dresser with a note that said, "I have served you well. Please release me," scrawled in her husband's hand. It didn't matter that while the person who lived there was packing, she moved an antique bench in her husband's office and found an old issue of *Premiere* magazine stuffed behind it with Kate Winslet on it, her bosoms appearing to be heaving so heavily they were on the brink of explosion. It did not matter, because when prospective buyers came to this house, that person was not going to be there. The lady who made crêpes on Sunday morning and who cooked with thirty-six-dollar olive oil would be.

The Fantasy Lady.

I called her Veronica.

Veronica was tall and slender, had beautiful, perfectly toned silver hair that she parted in the middle and tucked behind one ear. She wore sweater sets with the cardigan draped across her shoulders, and it never fell off. She had nicely defined upper arms and tapped a tiny silver spoon against the rim of her teacup when she was done stirring. She favored pale lipstick, and there was never dirt or traces of staph infections under her nails.

In short, basically, Veronica was not me. She didn't drink her tea out of a Bigfoot mug, eat dinner every night on the couch, or laugh when food fell out of her mouth. No one wanted to buy a house from a dirty pudgy girl.

But everyone wanted Veronica's house.

And even though Veronica's house was perfect in every way, from the matching white dishes that shone through the glass-fronted cabinet doors I had just finished putting up to the brand-new Roman shades I had installed in all bedrooms to the fresh sunflowers in an antique pitcher sitting on the dining room table, when the real estate agent saw it and agreed to put the house on the market the following Monday, I was still not prepared for what I saw on the front lawn the day the sign went up.

Oh my God, I thought. My house. *My house.*

In an instant, everything went blurry, my face got hot, and my throat closed up.

What was I doing? Was I out of my mind? "This is crazy," I said out loud. This is completely insane. I'm not moving. This is my house. My HUD house, my 1927 blond-brick bungalow that took almost a decade and every penny I had to make into Veronica's house. And in a move fed by emotion, I ran to the nearest doorway and put my arms on either side of the wall and my head against the inside of the doorjamb.

"What are you doing?" my husband said when he came home.

"Shut up!"

"Are you . . ." He lowered his tone. "Honey, are you hugging the house?"

"You're an asshole," I said, choking. "So what if I'm hugging the house!"

"I—" he started.

"It's my house! I can hug it if I want to!" I bellowed.

"You're crying," he replied gently. "What happened?"

"When I found this house it was brown on a dirt lot," I spewed. "And bums had been living in it and the kitchen counter had that awful brown tile and the floor had that asbestos flooring that I'm sure we both got cancer from when we took it up and there was no air-conditioning and it was so hot. It was so hot. And then I took eight layers of paint off the fireplace mantel and realized that was the only thing holding it together and I rebuilt it. And one night when you were late coming home I took a screwdriver and a hammer and chiseled away that brown tile in the kitchen and found soapstone. And under the asbestos was that tar-covered wood floor that you sanded for a month until it turned a honey color and it was just beautiful. And I found the swinging kitchen door in the barn and took eight layers of paint off that, too, but it took me six years to find the right piece of hardware for us to put it up with; I found it in that salvage place in Seattle. And I wrote three hundred product reviews about spatulas for Amazon to buy our air conditioner, and I was so sick of salad spinners and vegetable peelers and slotted spoons that I wanted to die, but we finally got air-conditioning and it was cool in the house for the first time ever, remember?"

As the tears rolled down my face, my husband looked at me, took my hand off the wall, and gave me a hug.

"I do remember," he said. "I remember when we thought it would be a good idea to sandblast the fireplace and within two seconds, the living room looked like a playground and the corner brick looked like it had a bullet hole in it."

I smiled. I nodded. "You're supposed to move the sandblaster around and not hold it in one place like you're peeing," I reminded him.

"I remember when you thought it would be a good idea to hire a homeless man to remove the dead trees in the front yard," he continued. "And I came home to a delusional, scabby schizophrenic running across my yard and then kung fu kicking the tree, like he was some sort of zombie Bruce Lee."

"I got in trouble for that."

"Yes, you did," he agreed. "And I remember a girl who wanted to save her house so bad she went out and fought a fire in her underwear, the ones that looked like a hula skirt. You could have and should have been arrested for indecent exposure, but that's how much you love this house. You risked being naked, *outside,* to protect it. I was in my underwear, too, so I just watched you from the bedroom window."

A laugh burst out of my throat.

"I *knew* I saw you in there," I said, breaking the hug. "I have to go out and look at the sign. I need to get this over with."

My husband followed me outside, and we stood together for a long time, just looking at the Realty Executives sign spiked in the middle of our front yard.

"I just can't believe we're doing this," I admitted. "I can't believe we're moving. I love this house."

"I love this house, too," my husband replied. "We'll get a great house in Oregon, I promise, but this will always be our first house. It will always be a special place for both of us."

"I forgot to tell you!" I suddenly said, remembering the police helicopter that had swooped in over my house at lunchtime. "A ghetto bird flew the lowest I've ever seen it today and shook the windows so hard I thought they were going to break! They must have been after someone good!"

"Well, I know it can't be anyone who has broken into our house, because they are invisible to law enforcement agents," my husband said.

"Oh my God!" I said as I began jumping up and down, barely able to contain my glee. "Maybe it's the sex offender! Maybe they've finally come for Kenny Ray!"

"Oh!" my husband suddenly remembered. "I forgot to tell you that when I was walking Bella in the park this morning—"

"She stopped and took a crap in front of the gang members sitting at the picnic table who snickered at you until she finished?" I asked eagerly.

"No, we don't walk by the picnic tables anymore after that happened last week," he said, wagging his finger. "As the sun was rising at five-thirty, I came upon a very tall woman in a sequined dress who was standing at one of the community barbecues. As I passed, I noted that she was cooking her breakfast—what I thought was a steak, but as I got closer, it turned out to be a huge, inch-thick, shiny piece of bacon! Then she turned and said very invitingly, 'Good morning,' like Ginger from *Gilligan's Island,* but *if Ginger were a man.*"

I gasped.

"I cannot believe you saw a park tranny grilling bacon at the break of dawn," I said, moaning. "You see all the good stuff!"

"Speaking of seeing things, what's that shiny round thing over there in the corner of the yard?" he asked as he began to walk over to it and I followed the several steps it took to get there behind him.

"What is that?" I asked as we got closer.

"I think it's a car wheel," my husband answered as he stood over it.

"Okay, and what's that?" I said as I pointed to the sidewalk directly in front of us.

"Silly of you to ask," my husband said, shaking his head in disgust. "Can't you see that's a five-foot-tall hockey trophy sitting on a skateboard?"

"I see it now," I admitted. "It *was* silly of me not to realize there was an enormous sports trophy sitting in front of my house on a skateboard. Am I drunk? Did I just sniff too much glue? What is wrong with me? Why *wouldn't* a skateboard, a trophy, and a wheel be in my yard?"

"You would think that if someone was going to dump some stolen things in our front yard, they would at least give us some of our own stolen stuff back," he said as we headed toward the house.

"The bathroom sink would be a nice start," I added as I followed. "Why can't that pop up on a pair of roller skates next to my clay pot of pincushion flowers that was stolen on Mother's Day?"

"See?" my husband said as he suddenly stopped. "I know you're sad to leave this house, I know you love it, and I know how much it means to you. But there are lots of things we won't miss about living here, and in Eugene, let's make sure we buy a house where a fifty-pound clay pot with a cubic meter of dirt in it won't walk away with a little help from an asshole who didn't think ahead to call FTD, okay?"

Wait," I said, and pointed to the mass of stolen loot heaped in our front yard. "What should we do about that? Should we bring them to the alley?"

"Are you kidding?" my husband answered as he looked at me unbelievingly. "Have you learned nothing while living here? If we go inside and pretend we left it outside, another thief will be along momentarily and resteal it so we don't have to worry about dragging it back to the garbage."

He was absolutely right. Within the hour, the crap had vanished, clearly on its way to another front yard in another part of the neighborhood.

I nodded and smiled, but I couldn't help it.

I still wanted to hug the wall.

Apparently, having a FOR SALE sign in your front yard was akin to draping a banner over your roofline that proclaimed, "ATTENTION, PLEASE: Neighbors, friends, clientele of Crack Park, people driving by, folks walking their dogs, illegal aliens and countrymen: Kindly do everything within your power to ensure that we cannot possibly sell our house under any circumstance imaginable. Please. Your cooperation is appreciated."

As soon as that sign went up and prospective buyers made appointments to view the house, someone threw a car speaker through the window of my husband's truck, creating a glittery, shiny, massive pool of shattered, sparkling glass in front of our house. Dogs crapped in our yard in unprecedented amounts; beer bottles and cans were often aimlessly thrown onto the grass, while other receptacles, like syringes and condom wrappers, were neatly perched on the hedge. And a hooker in a fishnet tank top decided to tap a new, fresh market by setting up shop a block away and propositioned high school kids on their way home in the afternoon. A pack of wild dogs, led by a mean, stumpy corgi, began roaming the neighborhood and surprised my next-door neighbor by appearing in her kitchen and devouring the contents of a Purina bag after gaining access through her doggie door. And one day, as I was about to pull into my driveway, a goat ran in front of my car.

"I can't sell my house if you aren't keeping tabs on your livestock and your herds!" I screamed at the top of my lungs to no one as I slammed my car door and trudged into my house in a goat rage. I was about to call my husband and scream about the goat encounter as soon as I threw my house keys and a new bouquet of brilliant sunflowers on Veronica's perfect dining room table when through the living room window I saw a German shepherd assuming the position on my lawn, which we had just paid to have fertilized and cut.

"Jesus Christ," I hissed through clenched teeth as I swung open the door and marched outside to my front porch, where I saw a blond woman standing by patiently as her dog defiled my thirty-dollar-a-week grass.

"Hi!" I called out to her cheerily as I waved and walked down the steps toward her.

"Hi," she replied without the enthusiasm I had reserved for my salutation.

"Can I have your address?" I asked with a big smile as I got close enough to her to push her down.

"Why?" she asked with a squint.

"Oh," I said, laughing. "Because by my estimate, my dog will be ready to take a huge, stinking, big-ass shit in about an hour, and I want to take her to your house to do it. Okay?"

"Hey!" I called out after her as she and her reluctant dog, its hindquarters pinched, raced down the street. "If you're missing a goat, I think he ran off with the whore, but I'm sure they'll both come back as soon as they're done digesting their last meal!"

And spotting the FOR SALE sign in the front yard didn't merely energize perpetrators of random fecal vandalism, either. People from all over, including some of my neighbors, saw it as an open invitation to knock on my door and expect to be invited in and receive a tour of my house at any time of the day or night that was convenient for them. We found one couple and their friend hanging out on our front porch at ten-thirty one night after we got home from the movies. One lady popped up at 7 A.M. and pounded on the door so insistently that the only reason I got out of bed was because I thought my backyard was on fire again. At other times, I'd be out in the front yard getting the mail or picking up that day's shit deposit when someone merely walking by would stop to ask if he could "take a look around."

"Well, I'd have to chain up the pit bulls and lock up the python, and that means I've gotta find him first," I told one man who I suspected was not as interested in buying my house as he was in casing it. "Unless you can bench-press a car, 'cause if you can do that, you can probably peel him away from your neck as he's strangling the last breath out of you. Would you be willing to sign a waiver, because my old man's been drinking and at last look, he was juggling his guns again."

Liberties unbound themselves even further when prospective buyers were in my house with their Realtors unsupervised and behaved as if they were in a rented hotel room and they were in Guns N' Roses. I came home after Realtor appointments on several occasions to find the decorative foot of my claw-foot bathtub knocked off from where it had been cemented, footprints on my furniture from where someone had been standing, my area rugs pulled up and left there, and an open kitchen-cabinet door that revealed a twenty-five-dollar Williams-Sonoma cracker collection—"classic companions for artisanal cheeses"—that had been violated and was no longer pure.

What kind of person does that? I thought to myself as I felt my blood pressure shoot up, and I vaguely identified the smell of burned hair. What kind of person walks into another person's house and helps himself to snacks and destruction? *Those aren't even my crackers; those are Veronica's, and what if she was planning on having ladies from the club over later?*

"Don," I said to my Realtor over the phone, "would you please inform people that I would appreciate it if when they enter, they resist the overwhelming urge to browse around, test out the merchandise, and, most important, abstain from nibbling on a free lunch out of my cupboards and refrigerator? Where do these people think they are, Costco?"

"You're kidding!" Don replied, completely aghast. "I'm so sorry! I can't believe someone did that!"

"I was quite surprised myself. Some filthy goblin broke into my box of artisanal cheese crackers and ate a handful," I informed him. "There were crumbs all over the counter!"

"That's appalling," he agreed.

"Naturally, 'the Biscotti al Formaggio feature thin slices of hearth-baked bread that are dipped in melted butter, topped with Romano cheese and Italian herbs, then baked a second time until they achieve the perfect degree of crispness,'" I told him as I read the description off the attractive gift box that housed them. "I mean, what's next? I'm afraid I'm going to come home one day and Papa Bear is going to be in my bed. Waiting."

"I'll take care of it," Don promised, and I believed him.

But my faith quickly lost ground the next day as I was driving back home while another starving, nosy-bodied, sticky-fingered looky-loo pulled away from my house with her mouth suctioned around one of Veronica's fancy blue-glass bottles of purified water from the south of France.

I couldn't believe it. I was so angry, especially since Don was the one showing her the house. Was my house being mistaken for a hostel? Were people going to start asking for a test drive next, moving in for a couple days or week to see if it was a good fit? Should I supply clean towels and soap in case someone wanted to freshen up? This was getting ridiculous.

"Don," I said firmly into the receiver, "I am not running a bed-and-breakfast here. I just saw that woman chugging a five-dollar bottle of water as she left my house. If that's what she's doing in the wide open, I don't want to even know what she did behind the cover of a closed door. Please tell me she kept her pants buttoned the whole time."

"In the big picture, Laurie, a blue bottle of water is not a big deal, I promise," Don tried to reassure me, laughing. "Especially when the person drinking it just offered you full asking price for the house. I almost gave her your fancy crackers, but I wanted to keep them for myself, so she got the water."

I was stunned into complete silence. I wasn't sure what to say. She wanted to buy my house? She was going to buy my house, just like that? How could she do that, when I could still change my mind? I mean, all I needed to do was go outside and hire the next tweaker scratching himself that passed by to kick the sign down.

I wasn't ready for this. The house had barely been on the market for two weeks. I was expecting months, time I needed to hug walls and yell at goats and enjoy living in Veronica's house. Enough time to have more of my things stolen and for the police helicopter to wake us up at night, and I never thought I'd say this, but I needed to sweat more. Maybe even get another dehydration-related kidney stone. I needed to be so extraordinarily sick of this place that it was easy to leave it and never look back. Never be sorry.

And certainly, I was afraid of leaving my family, but my plan was, with the direct flight back and forth from Eugene and Phoenix, I would be able to fly in once a month. I would see my family a little less than I saw them now. Still, once I sold the house, it was gone. I could never come back again.

"Laurie," Don urged on the other end of the phone. "Did you hear me? She wants the house! You sold your house! Isn't that fantastic?"

I nodded, swallowing hard. "Yeah, that's great, Don," I said, trying to put a smile into my voice. "That's so great. Did she see the cat farm across the street, and the gang graffiti tagged on the fence? And that the neighbors on the corner park in their front yard? And then we have our own rapist."

"The corgi dog gang even chased her from her car to the front door," Don said excitedly. "She saw it all. She wants the house, and don't you even think about backing out. I'm making double commission on this, and I've already booked my cruise!"

* * *

I've never printed the pictures of the house we took on that last day.

I've looked at them once or twice, flipped through the folder I keep them in on my computer, but the emptiness that swallows the rooms catches me in the throat and makes my eyes burn. There's my husband and our dog, Bella, kneeling down in front of the fireplace and the built-in bookcases, smiling, the floor so shiny and wide behind them. Barnaby, our old, deranged cat, standing on the spot where he peed in his kitty bed and stained the floor in my office where I had just finished writing my fourth book. My deserted kitchen, the soapstone counter patterned with the reflections of the tree outside, and the cabinets free of even Veronica's things.

Everything looks so still in those pictures, like a house about to be left.

The woman who bought our house worked in historic preservation for the city, so I knew that she wouldn't gut the place and tear all the wonderful things about it out. She had just gotten divorced, and I was honest when I told her that the house would take care of her, because as much as we had taken care of it, it had taken care of us. Especially with the iron bars on the windows and doors and the crowbar I left on the windowsill.

The last picture I took of the house that day was from the sidewalk, and the sky is so blue and the sun so bright and shining that it makes everything look so magnificently clean. It makes it look brilliant. The grass had just been mowed, the stripes of each lawn mower pass are apparent, and there's not an errant piece of dog shit in sight. The sky is *so* blue, strikingly blue, and oddly enough, everything against it, the grass and the trees, looks amazingly green.

It was a lovely house, both Veronica's and mine.

"Did you want one last hug?" my husband asked as I got into the car, packed with Bella, Barnaby, her bed, his litter box, and everything else that was relevant for our three-day drive up to Eugene and our new apartment.

I shook my head. "No, that last one took up most of the morning, and I still have the imprint of the wall texture on my cheek," I said. "I think I'm good."

"You brought those fancy crackers, right?" he questioned. "I've never had crackers like that. They are so good!"

"I got 'em, they're in the back," I replied.

And with that, we pulled away from the curb of our house and headed toward the freeway, toward I-5 West.

Balls and Putters

One of the last things I heard on the Phoenix nightly news before I left was that a male-only golf course was being planned for Maricopa, a small desert town a couple of miles outside of Phoenix. Consequently, I have to admit that I was mad.

I was mad and offended, thinking that the whole thing smacked of sexism and inequality. I was imagining the male-only golf course in my head, picturing the fellas slapping each other on the back, remarking, "Listen to how quiet it is here without women! It's so peaceful! I haven't heard a sound since Bill's last burp and the splash of Bob's urine hitting that tree trunk. It's remarkable."

And then, all of a sudden, I realized that a male-only golf course was a miracle. A pure miracle! In fact, women have been waiting for this event for years, hoping it would come, looking toward the skies for a sign. And now the time had arrived.

Naturally, it had to be men who made the first move of boorishly excluding the other sex, mainly because most women are far too polite to do such a thing. We'd worry about hurting men's "feelings," completely forgetting that most men don't typically purchase the biological upgrade package that includes those options, although they'll fork over eighty thousand dollars for a lifetime membership to a men's only golf club. And now that it's done, now that the line of exclusion has been crossed, it opens everything else up. I hope you're ready, boys.

For starters, I'd like to suggest a female-only airline. I mean, imagine, ladies, actually utilizing an armrest that hasn't been staked out and claimed by a big man arm, despite the fact that half of it is legally yours. Imagine the luxury of never having the dimwit in front of you recline all the back into your lap because he's more self-absorbed than a Bounty paper towel and understands others around him merely to be props. Imagine a whole entire flight without getting kicked in the kidneys *once* by a Florsheim. And the peanuts would disappear, replaced lovingly by Ghirardelli chocolate squares.

Second, I'd like to propose women-only roads and freeways. Sure, you might get tailgated once in a while by a sister applying lipstick, but at least you can be fairly confident that when she passes you, there won't the barrel of a shotgun poking out her window with your forehead centered nicely in the scope. And if that isn't enough incentive, chances are that you'll never have to hear a Boston or Rush tune blaring out of the Firebird pulled up next to you, or the thumping bass in a rap song played so loud that the sound waves are strong enough to remove the plaque from your teeth.

Next, I'd like to submit the idea of female-only bars. Yes, I know that we already have some of those, but I'm talking about some that aren't so special-interest specific, I guess. Just a good old place where a girl can have a drink without anyone assuming that she used to work for Heidi Fleiss. It would also be nice to have a beer or two without hearing the words "High five!" and "Score!"

Now, a good majority of the offenses listed aren't committed by all men, just by the kind of guy who thinks that his golf club should only be open to half of the world's population. Unfortunately, however, it still means that all males would be excluded, not just the suckiest ones.

And just to make sure that no guys try to slip in, the security factor of nudity will be strictly enforced in all female-only areas, as will pillow fighting and brushing each other's hair.

Hope you fellows have fun with your balls and putters.

The Uhhhhhmazing Dr. Wells

When I saw the infant black hair attempting to sprout on my chin, I have to admit I felt a little excited flip in my stomach.

The time, I knew, was almost at hand. It was going to be nothing short of a massacre.

Six weeks earlier, I had gone to see my dermatologist, Dr. Wells, after I had noticed a weird freckle on my arm and decided to get it checked out. While I was waiting for him in the examining room, I took a look at all the medical things on the walls—pictures of carcinomas and other kinds of skin cancers; diagrams of blackheads, regular old pimples, and boils; photos of acne, both before and after treatment. Then one poster caught my eye: it was an invitation to the wonderful world of laser hair removal, where traces of my Italian heritage and simian DNA could be eradicated with one pass of a concentrated light beam.

I nearly gasped at the possibility and, from force of habit, touched my chin, which was almost always compulsively plucked, lest I ignore it for a week and allow my jawline to begin to resemble that of a Chinese emperor. I imagined it soft and whisker-free, never having to worry if a bristle had grown in overnight and flourished to its full three-inch potential, never having to attack a stubborn one with a wax strip enough times that it left me with a rug burn and the squatter hair still smack in the middle of it. I wanted the chin of a supermodel, or I wanted at least one of my chins to resemble a supermodel's—it didn't have to be all three of them.

I remember when I found my first little piggy chin hair. I was sitting Mrs. Gaio's senior-year high school English class, reading my part in *Macbeth* (I was ominously typecast as one of the witches), when I felt something pokey, yet flexible sticking out of my face, and I was so naïve and unspoiled that I actually thought it was a splinter. After class was over, I rushed to the bathroom to take a peek in the mirror and to my horror met the bane of my chin existence, which would taunt me for the next twenty-odd years. I was shocked when I saw that black sprout emerging from my skin. I actually recall my stomach becoming a cold pit of fear as I realized that the only explanation I could come up with was that I was a hermaphrodite, and that things would probably be getting much, much worse as other "parts" of me began to grow manly and I made the full transformation into a "shim." For the rest of the day I wallowed in the sick feeling that at any moment my voice might change and my ovaries might drop, and I was terrified of what I might find when I took off my bra that night.

See, because that is what happens when the fifth-grade PE teacher doesn't give you all the details, just the pretty sales pitch, suggesting that having a menstrual cycle is like having a time-share, and the rest of your life as a woman will be like a Dove commercial. Sure, the girls get the boilerplate lecture and film-strip about how becoming a woman is so magical and beautiful and silky, when really, they should be telling you that your days of living maintenance-free are quickly drawing to a close and that in no time at all, you'll be finding yourself clutching your abdomen in a Circle K in the dead of night with a churning uterus buying some super-absorbency tampons from a tweaker, having hot wax poured on places a gynecologist charges extra to go to, watching your boobs get flatter and longer, and waiting for your cookie to fall out, because yes, that can happen and I know *because I asked.* Give that thing enough of a workout and someday you'll be in Africa, picking it up out of the dirt with a stick, knowing it isn't a dream.

But then again, maybe you can't tell little girls things like that. Maybe you can't have a filmstrip full of ladies with beards, gray pubic hair, and boobs that start to look like pita bread, and as a result of this willful ignorance, maybe believing you're a hermaphrodite for a day is enough to terrorize anyone into understanding that a couple of goat hairs isn't such a big deal and to stop crying. Because I can honestly say that if I found out as an eleven-year-old that things like Brazilian waxes and surgically trimming one's labia would be not only done but societally encouraged in the not-so-distant future, chances are I would have lost the will to survive right then and there. I had enough problems just trying to remember to sit like a lady when wearing a skirt.

So, while delighted that I held my open houses during the nineties when going the extra mile in landscaping your private yard meant having used a brand-new razor and not in the current times when having a bleached anus would be listed in the "plus" column in the dating pool, I still had the chin hair to contend with, and when I saw the posters up in Dr. Wells's office, I nearly squealed like the little piggy whose chin I had. I had been far too sensitive and embarrassed to seek out a proprietor of such services on my own, but here it was, as good as being delivered to me on a surgical steel platter. When Dr. Wells's nurse came in to take my medical history, I jumped on the chance.

"I want laser hair removal. I know I'm here for the weird freckle, but I want laser hair removal instead. Can we do it? Can we do it today?" I asked frantically.

"Well," the nurse said, laughing, "it doesn't really work like that. We do the procedure on-site, but we have a technician who comes in once a month to operate the technical aspects of it, though Dr. Wells actually does the lasering. And . . . we currently have a long waiting list. It fills up pretty quickly. Where were you thinking of having it done—legs, bikini, breasts, anu—"

"God no!" I spat. "No. I have no desire for the physical attributes of a fetus. Besides, this property has been sold for quite a while, so I'm only interested in public areas, like my chin."

"Well, let's take a look," she said as she swung a bright light over and scanned my chin. "Hmmm. You pluck, correct?"

I nodded.

"In that case, it wouldn't be successful until the hair is grown out and visible, so I would say you could do your first session in about three months, and you can't pluck up until then."

"Oh, you're kidding," I moaned, knowing that the whole deal was off. "Forget it. I can't do that. I'd come back in three months looking like ZZ Top. I'd rather let my roots grow out than my circus-lady beard. I knew it was too good to be true."

"Now, wait," the nurse advised me. "You can't pluck because Dr. Wells needs to see the follicle he's zapping. But you can shave.

That would eliminate the length of the hair and keep the follicle intact."

Well, that would be delightful, I thought to myself. My biggest dream come true. I get to look at the mirror every day and shave my face like a boy on the cusp of manhood. Oh, good, maybe I'll get some pungent BO, contract athlete's foot, and stick a poster of Pamela Anderson behind my bedroom door, too, just to round out the picture.

"All right, I'll try to resist the urge," I pledged. "But I'm telling you, this is undiluted, professional-strength Italian body hair. I could weave baskets out of it."

And just then, a horrible, tragic thing happened.

The door swung open and in stepped Dr. Wells. The charming, bewitching, engaging, alluring Dr. Wells.

"Hello there, Miss Notaro!" he said as he swept into the room and cheerfully shook my hand.

Now, I wouldn't say that Dr. Wells was going to put Brad Pitt on the unemployment line, not at all. But I would say that with his friendly demeanor, his impeccable graying temples, and his twinkling, almost impish eyes, I could have developed a nice little crush on him. Not in a marriage-threatening, "How could you, I trusted you" sort of way, but in the same way you develop a crush on a nubile young starlet, insist on renting all the movies in which your crush appears, and when you're moving, your wife finds a *Premiere* magazine cover with the huge pumpkin-head face of the crush on it behind a bench in your office. I mean *that* kind of crush.

But I decided to suppress my potential and as of yet undeveloped infatuation-like feelings for Dr. Wells, because he was my doctor, and that would be inappropriate, plus I would not be surprised at all if he had simply bands of hirsute women clamoring after him and his warm, sparkly white smile and flawless skin. And perfectly graying temples.

Perfectly.

In addition, I knew that should I become even the slightest bit enamored of Dr. Wells, I would do something stupid and clumsy in front of him, thus changing his opinion of me forever and never allowing him to see the gentle, quiet, sad beauty that existed within me, encased in a tomb of prickly black splinters of chin hair that I had promised not to pluck.

So I made my appointment for the laser removal at the front desk after I paid for the checkup for the weird freckle, which turned out to be nothing but a weird freckle, and I waited.

When I saw the inklings that the first new chinny chin chin hair had arrived, I have to admit, I felt the flush of excitement. The time was almost at hand. The plan was falling into place. So I waited three months, kept my razor in the shower hidden under a wash puff lest my husband see it, since I'm pretty damn near positive Kate Winslet doesn't lather up and slide a blade across her face of questionable gender every day like a drag queen. By the time the three months was up and dots of tiny black sprouts had arrived on my chin en force, I entered the shower every morning looking like a Sharpie had attacked me during the night. My husband nicely refrained from pointing out that it was in my best interest as a werewolf to avoid full moons and crucifixes.

Then, just as Dr. Wells's business card that was held by a magnet to my refrigerator door told me, the day arrived for my laser hair-removal beautification to begin. I showed up on time, and the nurse took me back into a room that had a large stainless steel machine in it next to what looked like a dentist's chair.

Then the door opened and there he was, the curiously amazing Dr. Wells, who took one look at me with those magic man eyes and said, "Miss Notaro, how are you doing today?"

I was already at a disadvantage, aware that when I'm in a reclining position looking up, my neck fat has a tendency to arrange itself in a singular, arching tube, much like the neck of a walrus or sea lion. Knowing I didn't look my best, despite my meticulous application of newly purchased eye shadow, mascara, and lipstick, I attempted to deliver a demure smile to Dr. Wells, successfully refraining from being smitten at the same time.

"Hmmmm, let's take a look," he said as he bent down and examined the area in question. "Oh, I'll have no problem seeing those! I can see you've let them grow out for a while, so thank you!"

If "a while" means less than the time between sunrise and sunset, then so be it, I thought to myself as I nodded. Apparently, I sprout hair faster than John Travolta after a long weekend trip to the "spa."

"Now I'm going to place these on your eyes to protect them from the laser, and I'm going to apply some conducting gel over the area," he informed me, putting little yellow suntan-booth goggles on my face. "When I begin the procedure, it will feel like little pins, like acupuncture. Little pinches. After the laser pulses, you'll feel a cooling sensation in the same spot. Are you ready?"

Then someone spackled some very chilly gel basically everywhere from my eyes down, and I braced myself for the first pinch, because when medical professionals tell you that something is going to "pinch," what they really mean is "This is going to feel like I made a shiv out of a rusty can and am going to ram it mercilessly into your kidney. So just relax."

I heard the *whirr* of the machine and braced myself for the pain of what I imagined would be like having a jumper cable touch my jaw, but surprisingly, it was relatively benign. It felt like a little, tiny jab with a pin, and I was amazed at how little it actually did hurt; right after the jab, I felt a very cold sensation. This whole laser thing was a breeze!

"Miss Notaro," I heard Dr. Wells say as gently as he could, "I know you are in here for the chin area, but I'm noticing substantial growth on the upper lip, and since we're already in process, we might as well tackle that too."

I wanted to gasp I was so embarrassed. I mean, having a little chin growth is one thing, but I had no idea I had a goatee going on. And apparently it was not merely "going on" but was *substantial.* Not peach fuzz, not one or two stray hairs, but the foundation for a handlebar sort of extremity. With a little bit of wax and some sculpting, who knew what I was capable of? I could hire myself out to fire stations and simply stand on the banks of a flash flood, rescuing people who rushed by in the torrent with merely a toss of my head. And poor Dr. Wells, who I'm sure thought his one-thirty appointment was to laser a woman and not Burt Reynolds, had no idea that he was going to need a rideable lawn mower to tackle the effects of my hormones.

Where is the miracle of spontaneous combustion when you need it? I thought to myself, and then suddenly, my breath was gone. Just gone. I was completely out of air, like something had quickly stolen it right out of me, like I was suffocating.

"UUUUUUHHHHHHHHHH," I heard myself emit quite loudly as my lungs desperately and in a panic tried to suck in a breath.

Oh my God, what was that? I asked myself.

"UUUUUUHHHHHHHHHH," I heard myself gasp again. It was the same sound you'd expect to hear if, say, you'd been partaking of a Tootsie Pop and it unexpectedly became disengaged from its stick body, rolled down your throat like a bowling ball, and then got lodged there. Like a plug. The sound you would make if that happened was the precise sound I was making, minus the Tootsie.

Shut up! *Shut up shut up shut up!*

The sound of the machine quickly stopped as Dr. Wells pulled off my yellow goggles.

"Miss Notaro, are you all right?" he asked, seeming very concerned.

"Well, I—that thing, I don't know what it is because I can't see it, but the cold thing is sucking the air out of my nose," I replied, trying to explain, because it was. Every time that little vacuum thing got close to a nostril, it felt as if I was drowning and couldn't get enough air.

"That's impossible," the gentle doctor explained. "It's blowing cold air out, not sucking air in. Are you in any pain?"

"No, not at all, I'm fine," I tried to reassure him. "I'm fine. You can keep going. I'll try to hold my breath."

Then, as soon as the machine turned back on, I felt a pinprick, the cold, and "UUUUUUHHHHHHHHHH," I gasped involuntarily, deep and raspy, as the sensation I felt was remarkably similar to the one I felt when I was ten, wanted to be an Olympic gymnast, and would repeatedly run across our yard and attempt to do a front flip but like the spaz I was would land flat on my back with the wind knocked right out of my lungs on a pool raft I was using for a mat. I would lie there, gasping for breath, as my mother looked out the sliding glass doors, yelling, "You're an idiot, you know! Gymnasts don't have legs that touch in the middle!" and then I'd get up and run across the yard again toward the pool raft.

"UUUUUUHHHHHHHHH," I heard myself bellow again, like a water buffalo calling for her calf.

The machine shut off again.

"Miss Notaro, I don't want to continue if this is causing you discomfort," Dr. Wells said frankly.

This time I took the goggles off, trying very hard not to imagine myself with my facial hair poking up out of the shiny gel that was smeared all over my face like a glazed donut, gasping uncontrollably like a halfwit writhing on a river raft in the dirt and doing it all wearing tiny yellow goggles.

"Really, I'm okay," I said again. "Maybe it's the shock of it being so cold that it's just a reflex, but I am completely fine and we have a mustache to conquer. Please pay no attention to it. Please."

Honestly, I couldn't believe that I was the only person in the history of mankind to act like I was getting strangled while being lasered for a biker mustache, but I knew all too well that now I was going to become "a story." I was going to be the story that Dr. Wells would tell his wife when he got home that night, the story that the machine technician would tell his co-workers and that the nurse would warn him of the afternoon of my next appointment. I was going to be remembered at this doctor's office, and let me tell you, I've worked in a doctor's office, they see a lot of people each day, and that includes a standard, expected percentage of nuts. The "stories" I remember from my doctor's office days are the lady who called and said she couldn't find her contact lens in her eye and was convinced it had worked its way out of the eye socket and lodged itself in her brain; the man who called and said he thought he had put eyedrops in his eyes, but it turned out to be Super Glue; and the man who entered the office dressed in a filthy sheet, a crown of ocotillo thorns and sandals, then raised his arms and declared that he was Saint Peter Christ, and I just might have believed part of his story had he not smelled quite so much like residual urine and tooth decay. That's what you experience when you work at a doctor's office; it just comes with the territory. So I know that if you're remembered, that means that you were coloring so far outside the normal freak lines that you get placed in a special category, reserved for the . . . special. In fact, I knew that by the time I left the office, I was already going to have a name.

The Heave Ho.

The Pant-y Waste.

H.R. Huff and Puff.

I took the deepest breath I possibly could and held it.

The machine began to whir again.

"UUUUUUHHHHHHHHHHH."

"UUUUUUHHHHHHHHHHH."

"UUUUUUHHHHHHHHHHH."

Finally, when Dr. Wells turned off the machine for good and

pronounced the session completed, he slapped both of his hands onto his legs and said, "Well, see you in six weeks, Miss Notaro."

Then he handed me a paper towel to wipe the gel off, got up, and left the room without looking at me once.

Wait! I wanted to shout. Just give me time! I know I can do it! *I know it.* Whatever. What*ever.* And you know what? I don't believe that no one else hasn't gulped! It was like being waterboarded! It was like having a Dyson stuck under my nose—of course I gasped! I'm surprised brain matter didn't fly out! It was like the car-wash vacuum. I *know* other people have gasped! It would be inhuman not to!

But I didn't say any of that. I just sat there, with shiny laser gel smeared all over my face as everybody left the room but me. Then I wiped the gel, of which there was so much I looked like I had just been attacked by a space creature, off my face, and that took a long time, because I didn't want the Heave Ho to walk out into the hallway and make her next appointment at the reception desk looking like a newborn Krispy Kreme rolling down the conveyor belt.

But apparently, news of my One Woman Chin Fringe show had already spread to the front office, and it was obvious as the girl who worked up there swiped my Visa and gave me an odd, insincere smile. She already knew. I smiled tightly, nodded to myself, and signed the receipt. Great. Three months of secret shaving in the shower only to have an even bigger humiliation in front of the charming and beguiling Dr. Wells, who I had once, approximately fifteen minutes ago, almost had a crush on. But no more, no more. No way. Obliterated like a follicle in the path of a laser beam. Vaporized. Dissolved! The receptionist had just handed me the receipt, and I was about to walk away, when suddenly Dr. Wells appeared and said something to the receptionist about a later appointment. This was my last chance, I knew, to show him that I wasn't a nut and that I was just a normal girl with an extra hormone or two.

Be normal, I told myself. Don't do anything doltish. Stay inside the lines. Be nice. Be normal. Smile big like nothing weird happened in there, like it was all cool and very routine.

"Thank you, Dr. Wells," I said as he looked up to catch my big, normal, nice smile. "I'll see you in six weeks!"

At first, Dr. Wells didn't say anything. He just looked at me without any expression on his face at all, not really staring but looking and not saying a word, which I guess could be classified as staring.

See, I thought to myself, almost pleased and even a little bit surprised. I can still cast a man spell! I smiled wider.

"Yes," he said suddenly, as if he just caught himself. "Yes, um, six weeks."

And on that note, I waved slightly, then turned and walked away. Now I need to spend the next six weeks practicing holding my breath with a vacuum-cleaner nozzle under my nose, I thought to myself as I sashayed to my car, so I can show him that *I can do it. Because I know I can. I know I can.*

Once I was in the front seat, I finally allowed myself to feel my chin and see just what a master Dr. Wells was, and as it turned out, he was a pretty good one. My chin felt smooth and stubble-free, just as I had hoped, so smooth and perfect, in fact, that I wanted to see it for myself.

I reached up to angle down the rearview mirror, but before I could study my beautiful new chinny chin chin, something caught my eye. Something reddish, something bold, and something that was covering every part of my face where the conducting gel had been. It was faint in some areas and stronger in others, across my chin, cheeks, my upper lip, my jawline, all over. It was spread like a virus, smeared to every inch of my lower face.

How could I have known?

It would have been impossible.

How could I have known that when you take conducting gel, mix it with pretty new and meticulously applied lipstick, and wipe it all over your face vigorously with a paper towel, you can make a nice, big red crazy clown mask with very little effort at all.

Very little.

"UUUUUHHHHHHHHHHH" was all I could manage.

Hit

We had just sat down on the steps of the amphitheater where the Indian Festival was being held when someone threw a water balloon at us.

I looked up immediately and searched the crowd, looking for the culprit or a suspicious movement that would lead me to his trail, but absolutely nothing looked out of the ordinary. There was just a bunch of people milling around as several young girls did a Bollywood-type dance on the stage before us. It was if the perpetrator had simply vanished.

Both Jamie and I had been looking forward to the Indian Festival for weeks, and I had driven up to Portland, where my friend had just moved, to stay the weekend, in order to take in everything the festival had to offer. Our mouths watered at the thought of golden samosas lining every pathway, chicken makahni flowing like rivers, and mango lassis bubbling out of water fountains. Once we walked onto the square where the festival was being held, there was no doubt as to what we were going to do first, and that was to get ourselves some vittles. Everything smelled so good; wafts of garlic, curry, and spices made my mouth instantly

water. I was so hungry. Jamie, her husband, and I had starved ourselves all day so we could be sure of gorging in nothing short of
copious Roman amounts, but when we arrived at the food court,
we were shamefully unprepared for the choices that lay before
us. In every direction, lines for food grew by the moment, so we
made a decision based on the apparent happiness of people leaving the booth with their food, and jumped in a line, watching it
grow five more feet behind us in a matter of a minute.

"What are you going to get?" I asked Jamie as we squinted to
see the menu far ahead of us.

"I think there's a combo plate," Jamie said, standing on tiptoe.
"But I'm so hungry I'd eat anything!"

"I am ravenous," I proclaimed.

"Ooooh," my best friend cooed as a lady with a combo plate
walked past us. "Look at that!"

"Even the smell is worth the wait!" I added. "I am *so hungry*.
I think my stomach just shrank to the size of an empty balloon!"

"Hang on," Jamie encouraged me. "We'll get there, and when
we do, we'll be feasting on something like that!"

A man and his little boy passed by, their plates piled with
steaming hot pakoras and samosas.

"Oh my God, that looks so good," I whined. "Little boy, I'll
buy you a bike for a bite!"

"Look, the line is moving fast," Jamie lied. "We'll be up there
in no time."

It was a lie. She knew it, I knew it, her husband knew it. I tried
to busy myself watching the crowds, clapping along with the little
dancers onstage, but all I could do was smell incredible food and
feel my stomach shrivel like a Shrinky Dink on a cookie sheet.

When we had been on line for a half an hour, Jamie turned around and whispered sharply. "I can hear you above the crowd! Maybe you should find a bathroom!"

"I am not farting," I replied. "That is the sound of my tummy crying."

Just then, a large family in front of us suddenly stepped out of line and there we were, at the counter. Face-to-face with the menu on a poster board. Within arm's reach of what we had waited so long for. We placed our orders for three combos, and within seconds they were delivered to the counter, like a reward for our tested patience.

Delighted and excited beyond belief, we navigated through the crowd with plates in hand, careful, oh so careful, not to spill so much as a drop. We made our way up the narrow steps of the amphitheater, found a perfect spot on one of the landings right in front of the stage, and sat down.

It smelled *so good*. With fork in hand I dug in for the first bite and savored it, no longer obsessing about the half-hour wait. I looked at Jamie and her husband, and they were both smiling after their first bites, too, and we all nodded. It tasted as good as it smelled; it was everything I had hoped for, everything that I had starved myself for in anticipation.

And then, as I was going in for the second bite, I felt something wet splatter on me, and automatically recoiled.

It was the water balloon. My first response was to search the crowd for the wake of a fleeing perp, but there was nothing. No heads turning, no sounds of running feet, no after-vandalism laughter.

I turned to Jamie with a look that said, "Can you believe it?" and that's when I saw that she had gotten the worst of it. Long, brown streaks covered her white T-shirt on the side closest to me. Brown, I thought to myself; why is the water in the water balloon brown? It was a mud balloon? How do you even make a mud-water balloon? How despicable! How sinister! How crafty! I'm going to have to try this at home!

The look on Jamie's face turned from surprise to horror as she studied her own shoulder and arm, and I scrambled for a napkin to help clean it off.

"Who would throw a water balloon?" I said angrily. "I didn't see anyone, did you? Did you see anyone throw it at us? Why would someone do that?"

And when I reached to get the mud-balloon residue out of her hair, I realized it.

My mind flashes to a college-aged Laurie who is sitting on a bench at Arizona State University, trying desperately to impress the guy she has successfully, after many months of trying to capture his attention, lassoed into being her Italian-language partner, when she feels a pinecone hit her in the head and the guy, duly impressed, begins to gag and then runs off, but not before uttering the words, "Rabies, typhoid and cholera."

To a thirtyish Laurie eating lunch with all of her new friends from the newspaper at a Mexican restaurant with outdoor seating when she is suddenly struck in the temple with a water gun as her new pals immediately shoot away from the table, muttering phrases such as "meningitis," "encephalitis," and a personal favorite, "bubonic plague."

And finally, to a scene in Laurie's bathroom in which a tiny, trapped baby bird craps all over her toothbrush as if it were a pterodactyl, bird feces the consistency of Liquid Paper, which then turns crumbly, then quickly solidifies into a sort of poo concrete.

Like the stuff that was now hardening in Jamie's hair.

"Oh my God," I said as I sucked air in. "Bird flu!!"

But honestly, in the times that I've been a victim of the skies, it was from a pinecone and water gun roughly the size of a pigeon and not an even more foul, more dastardly, and more disease-ridden seagull circling, scouring the Indian Festival for just the right head to shit on.

Locating the shiniest and happiest head, the filthy seagull released its load on Jamie, who, to her credit, did not freak out the way you would suppose a person who's been emptied on would. She just looked at me with disgusted eyes and said simply, "It stinks."

There really wasn't anything she could do; she just sat there as her husband and I tried to wipe the slime off of her, to very little avail. If you've ever been pooped on, you already know that your options are rather limited unless you have a bottle of Clorox, a wire brush, and some hair clippers at your disposal, although some radiation treatments would also be handy. Jamie had been a victim in one of the highest levels of a Conflict With Nature, only to be topped by a bear sucking the bone marrow out of your spine or a lion picking its teeth with your ribs. There is very little else nature can do to you to let you know that the human race is just another gobbling, roaming, feral group of creatures on this planet, and that where the universe is concerned, there is no first class. Everybody gets a fair shot with a pinecone to the head, a water balloon to the shoulder, and it can be when you're trying to impress a boy or having lunch with your friends, although in my experience, two out of three bird poopings have taught me that you're far more likely to encounter a free-roaming shitstorm when you're eating delicious, ethnic food under a tree. Just my two cents.

As we wiped her down, Jamie sat there like a volcano, boiling inside but calm on the exterior, watching the little girls dance on-stage and holding her plate of food that was no longer steaming.

Oh no, I thought suddenly as I grabbed her plate, studied it, then grabbed my own, which I had set down beside me.

It was true. Not only had the bird soiled my best friend, but it had released its intestinal cargo on our chicken makahni, on our vegetable korma, on our delicately fried pakoras like it was a curry Porta Potti. I pulled the plate away from her longing eyes, and pulled it out of the hand of her husband, who, fork poised, was going in for another mouthful.

"Awwwww," he moaned as I plucked it from his tightening fingers. "Come on! Can't we just eat around it?"

"You are a *medical doctor*!" I reminded him. "I have substantially fewer diseases than that foul bird. If I crapped on your food, would you eat around *that*?"

My best friend's husband looked at me and then looked at Jamie with a "Why is she here?" expression.

With sincere regret and anguish, four steps, and a very unceremonial, craptastic *plop!*, our chicken-poop combos went straight into the trash, never to be heard from again.

"I stink!" Jamie said angrily, trying to look over her shoulder to take a gander at the stains that striped her back. "The smell is making me want to hurl. I'm going to throw up if I don't get this off of me. I need new clothes, and I need them now. *And by the way, I'm still hungry!*"

I didn't want to say anything, but I was still hungry, too. I had only managed to get a bite or two of my combo down before the attack occurred, and honestly, no matter how hungry I was, I would begin to eat things from my own body before thinking that eating off of that plate was anything less than parasitic suicide.

Luckily for us, there was a sportswear store directly across the street from the festival, where salespeople kept asking me how I was doing while Jamie tried on T-shirts, and I got to say three times, "I'm great, but my friend just got defiled by sky turds," but no one seemed to think that was out of the ordinary, they just smiled and nodded, or maybe they thought I was homeless, since I am sure I had that hungry, deranged "I'll do anything for saag paneer, I'll pave you a driveway or grant you a wish! Any wish!" sort of look.

My stomach, by that time, had flipped itself inside out and was hopping around my abdominal cavity like a trout on the deck of a boat. My eyes had gotten quite wide, my belly was getting extended and round like a basketball, and flies were starting to land on me, *I was that hungry.* Jamie emerged from the dressing room wearing the new, clean shirt, paid for it, and then we headed back over to the Indian Festival.

Redemption waited for us somewhere on another food line, I knew it, but to my horror, the lines hadn't gotten any shorter—in fact, they had grown since our first visit to the food court. The three of us, by this time, were depraved, haunted souls, eager to take any food and just be satisfied with it. We chose the shortest line and hopped onto it silently. Every two to three minutes we'd take a step forward, a step closer to placing our order.

We waited on that line for a very, very, very long time, and this time, we didn't look on happily as people passed us with their food, smug and arrogant as they were, the prickly bastards. So proud they had food. "Look what we've got!" their bright, stupid eyes said. "We've got food!" *Yeah, well, we had been there. We had food.* We were actually *eating*, sitting down and eating, not that you'd know it by looking at our pallid complexions, our sallow cheeks, and our thin, pursed lips, only to be forced by nature's cruelty and a leaky fowl bowel to stand in line all over again.

"What are you getting this time?" Jamie asked me weakly as she swatted a fly away.

"I dunno," I replied, barely audibly. "Maybe some rice. Broth, if they have it. It's been such a long time since I've eaten that I'm not even sure my system can take it."

"Look at that," she noticed, and pointed with a limp hand at me. "I think one of your collarbones just surfaced, like a submarine."

I nodded. "I'm going through my reserves quickly," I agreed. "They've been buried under a layer of fat permafrost since the 1990s. God. If I start seeing the bones in my feet, I know I won't have long to go. I'll tell you right now, if someone drops a piece of naan, I'm going for it. I won't eat bird shit, but I will eat shit off the ground."

Then, finally, we were at the front of the line, and as Jamie and her husband were getting ready to order, holding out their cash, an old, horrible hag stepped in front of us and began screeching like a gorgon.

"This isn't the paying line! This is the ordering line! You need a token! A token! You have to stand on that line to get a token first, and then you wait on this line to order!" she warbled like the nasty old biddy she was, waving around her stupid blue token like it was a flag.

Jamie ignored her, pushing past, and gave the food vendor her order. The old hag stood in front of Jamie's husband, clearly trying to block him from going any further.

"That's my wife, and she's already ordered my food," he said, trying to reason with the old woman, who must have known she was no match for him. She stepped aside, and as she did, something of a floodgate opened. People from the very poorly marked token line began to swarm in front of me and actually physically pushed me completely out of line.

I stood there, not really knowing what to do. It had happened as quickly as that, and suddenly the line was not a line but a bulge of people trying to hand someone a stupid token and order some food. The next thing I knew, Jamie and her husband were standing next to me with two new plates of food, and honestly, I couldn't do it again. There was no way I could get in the back of the token line, which didn't remotely resemble a token line, by the way, but looked like just a regular old line, and wait one more time. I was just all waited out.

As we walked out of the food court, trying to find a covered place to eat, I saw the old biddy ahead of us a couple of steps, not even waiting to sit down before she dug in. She shoved food into her mouth like it was a dump, and at this point, I knew what I wanted most in the world. I didn't want naan, or a pakora, or some saag paneer. No I didn't. I wanted to take five steps ahead, pop the bottom of her plate up like it was a tambourine, snap off her head, rip out her spine, and start sucking the bone marrow out of it. That's exactly what I wanted to do.

But as we passed her on the way to a spot beneath an over-hang, I looked at her kindly, and with a big smile I said, "I really hope a bird shits on you. And I mean aaaallllllllllllllllllllllllllllllllll over you."

And lady, if you're reading this, you'd better know that we're not done, you and I. We're not done. I remember your face, I re-member that pinchy, wrinkly cavern of a mouth, I remember your purple and blue Bossy Old Lady–issue rain jacket, and somewhere, somehow, you and I will be in line together again, if I have to go to every food-related festival in the general vicinity to track you down. I will see you in line, somewhere, somehow, and when I do, I will swiftly and stealthfully exact my revenge, even if it calls for bringing my own pooping bird to season all of your food.

As Jamie and her husband ate their food in a parking garage across the street and I stood next to them, I made a mental note: If we do this again next year, I gotta remember to bring an um-brella and pack a lunch.

Ready or Not

I **knew right away** that she was the one.

"That one." I pointed at the computer screen to my husband, who was looking over my shoulder.

"Hmmmm, I don't know," he said cynically, and I knew he wasn't kidding.

"That's her," I insisted, knowing that I was not going to take no for an answer. "That is my dog!"

"We'll see," he said, like he had any power over the decision. "We'll talk about it when I come home."

I didn't say anything. I didn't even look at him.

"Laurie," he said firmly—and that's when I know he's really mad, because he never says my name unless I've pissed him off enough that he actually has to spend the energy to remember it— and turned me around by the shoulder. "I'd better not come home and find that dog here. I mean it. This is something that we need to talk about first."

"Fine," I said as I shrugged, then turned back around to look at the photo on the monitor.

"I mean it," he said again before he headed out of my office and left the house for school.

I knew that little dog on the county pound site was my dog. I just knew it.

I knew it in the same way I knew it when I first saw Bella, five years earlier, a shivering, screeching, wet little puppy clawing at the gate to her cage where she sat all alone, the only one of her litter not yet adopted. She looked like a little red rat, although the animal attendant assured me she was of German shepherd lineage. Honestly, she could have been a jackal with hair poking out of her red-stained teeth and we still would have taken her home. She was all alone and scared to death. You would have had to be soulless to pass that puppy up, with her tiny red velvet mouth and her huge brown eyes outlined in black that looked like Maybelline eyeliner. We knew we had found our girl.

She couldn't have behaved better on the drive up to Eugene from Phoenix, especially since we were in the car nine hours a day and she was forced to share space with the cat, who farted, squeaked, and hissed his way the fifteen hundred miles there, despite my best efforts to chew up a tablet of Dramamine for him like a mother bird since all of his teeth were gone and and I wanted to keep him as drugged up as possible.

But Bella was a dream, and to be honest, I was a little worried. Six months before our move, my brother-in-law had been over at the house, picked up one of her balls, and thrown it into the air in front of her.

"That dog can't see," he said a moment after he caught it.

"That's ridiculous," I pooh-poohed him. "Of course she can see. We play ball every day."

"Well, look at her," he said as he threw the ball up in the air again and caught it, as she sat, looking straight on. Her eyes never moved. She just stared straight ahead.

"That's crazy," I said again. "I swear I play ball with her every day."

But he was right. I saw that for myself as I followed him out to the backyard and he threw the ball, and I watched Bella, who waited to hear it bounce and then shot in the right direction. And after several appointments with her vet, then a doggie eye specialist and numerous tests, including one that involved attaching feelers to her eyes and measuring her reaction to lasers, it was determined that Bella had sudden acquired retinal degeneration syndrome and wasn't entirely blind but had only about 20 percent of her vision left. And that, I was told, wouldn't last much longer. In just a short period, she would be completely blind.

I felt like someone was playing a bad joke on us, and I still had trouble believing it. She didn't bump into furniture; she ran around the backyard; she even chased after balls. Bella could catch a French fry when I tossed it at her. What blind dog does that? I insisted to the vet, hoping to catch him in a web of his own very expensive "let's hook your dog's eyeballs up to sensors and spin a disco ball at her" lies.

Her vision had degenerated over several months, I was told, and as that happened, her other senses, particularly smell, became sharper. She knew the layout of the furniture and the house, and she'd adapted. She could *smell* a French fry coming at her. She could *hear* where the ball went.

"Don't feel sorry for her and let her just lie around the house all day," the specialist urged. "She's not feeling sorry for herself. She's using what she's got to get along."

And that's when I decided that if my dog could do that, if she could catch a French fry in the dark, then she could do anything. So I decided to become Bella's Seeing Eye person, and we went straight home and started working on "up." Down. Forward. Left. Right. And she learned all of it. I searched out toys that made noise, bought anything with a bell on it, and dabbed them with scented oils to help out a little more.

Bella did great. I wouldn't say she was a natural at being blind, but she adapted better than I could have ever hoped for. I took her off commercial dog food and started making her dinner, and I researched supplements and vitamins that were thought to improve vision. Though the specialist said she would be completely blind within weeks, when we got to Oregon six months later, she still retained a substantial amount of her sight.

We had been in our apartment for about three weeks when one night Bella didn't eat her dinner, didn't even seem interested.

"Come on," I tried to coax her from where she lay resting on the floor. "There are eggs in it, and green beans, and a bunch of hamburger. Yummy!"

She looked at me but didn't move.

"Maybe she's bored with it," I assessed. "I should have made her chicken."

"Come on," my husband said, laughing. "If she won't eat that, I will!"

"Maybe she doesn't feel good," I said. "Maybe she has a cold or something."

"Give her a cookie," my husband urged. "See if she'll take a treat."

I got a liver treat, her favorite, from the pantry and offered it to her. She moved her head to look at it but didn't sniff it, then moved her head away.

And that was our first sign that something was wrong. By the next morning, she wouldn't even get up. I grabbed our vet's list of recommended animal hospitals in Eugene—we hadn't even been there long enough to have a new vet. I called the closest one as soon as they opened the next morning, and they agreed to see her right away.

"Why isn't she walking?" Dr. Greer asked when he saw my husband carry her into the office.

"She can't get up," I said, thinking that in a minute it would all be fine. In a minute Dr. Greer would be able to fix her and then I could give her a cookie and we could take her home and laugh about what a lazy little dog she was, making us carry her into the vet!

He took some blood, then went into the back to analyze it. When he returned, he took a deep breath. "She's anemic," he said, and I breathed a huge sigh of relief.

Thank God, I thought. Barnaby's anemic. All we have to do is give her some medication and she'll be fine. She's just tired. Thank God.

"Her red blood count is very low," he said slowly. "It's at sixteen."

"Okay," I said, nodding along. "Okay, so what can we give her for this?"

Dr. Greer was quiet for a moment. "No," he said, barely shaking his head. "At twelve, death occurs. I'm going to send this blood work up to a lab in Portland. It could be caused by a parasite, cancer, or autoimmune disease."

"She wasn't sick yesterday," I insisted. "She was fine yesterday. We played ball, we went on a walk. She wasn't sick yesterday. We were at the beach this weekend; she ran all over the place."

The vet said that Bella was also dehydrated and that he wanted to keep her at the office to give her some fluids and for observation until the test results came back that afternoon. To be truthful, I was angry; I knew all too well that our vet in Phoenix had his own lab attached to the practice, and we would have had results in a matter of minutes. There wouldn't have been any waiting and second-guessing. But no. We had to move to a town so goddamned small that it didn't even have a lab, couldn't even tell us what was wrong. This would have never happened in Phoenix. It would have never happened.

He sent us home and said there was nothing for us to do but wait to hear from him.

By six that night, we still didn't have any results, but Dr. Greer suggested that we move Bella to the emergency animal hospital that opened at six-thirty. He had already called over and explained the situation, he told me, and he recommended that Bella receive a blood transfusion. Her red blood cell numbers had dropped again.

"You're a good girl," I said, holding her in the back of the car as my husband navigated the dark, rainy streets of a new town we didn't know. "You're a good girl, and we love you so much."

Bella raised her head and licked my hand.

When we pulled into the parking lot, several vet techs and the vet on duty were waiting at the door for us, and they took Bella from my husband and carried her to the back.

"She's blind," I called out after them, something that I realized I didn't even think about anymore, it was just the way we were.

I felt a tear slip down my face. And then another, and then another. My husband took my hand. The room became blurry, and the other people in the waiting room looked away.

• • •

At six the next morning, the phone rang loudly, and I froze. I held my breath as my husband answered it, then exhaled when I saw a smile stretch across his face.

"She's doing good!" he whispered to me as the emergency vet told him that the transfusion had gone really well. Her red blood cell numbers were back up. She hadn't eaten but she'd drunk some water. She was alert, they said. Come down and see her.

And when we got there, Bella stood up and wagged her tail at the sound of my voice. We were petting her through the wire door when the vet came over and opened it for us. We both hugged her.

"She's so happy you're here," the vet said. "She still needs quite a bit of rest. She's not out of the woods yet, but things are looking up."

I was thrilled. I couldn't wait to take her home. I handed the techs the container full of Bella's food that I had brought, hopeful that she might eat something. I could tell that she was still so tired, but at least she was standing up and wagging her tail.

"Let's let her rest," the vet recommended after several minutes. "Come back at about noon and you can visit again."

My husband and I were both smiling when we left. I wanted to skip to the car. Bella was going to be okay. She'd be back home in a couple of days. I felt elated. I loved that little dog. She was the only friend I had in this new little town. We only had each other so far.

We went back home, and made breakfast, delighted that she'd soon be joining us. Barnaby, on the other hand, took advantage of her absence and demanded some one-on-one cat time.

Minutes before noon, I had just put on my coat and grabbed the keys to the car to head out to the animal hospital when the phone rang again. My husband answered it and listened intently for a moment, then slammed down the receiver.

"We've got to go," he said, running for the door. "It's the vet. They're losing her. We have to get there now."

• • •

"Go faster," I said quietly, staring at the car in front of us. "You have to go faster."

"It will be okay," my husband said as if to reassure himself. "We'll get there in time. We will. We'll get there in time."

I didn't ask what the vet had said exactly. I didn't want to know. I wanted simply, purely, to get there in time. That's all. That's all either one of us wanted. I didn't want her to be alone.

My husband swerved into the parking lot and stopped the car; we flew out of it and ran toward the animal hospital door.

I saw a vet tech rushing into the waiting room, and as I frantically opened the door and rushed inside, I heard someone yell, "Don't let them back here!"

"My dog," I said, looking at the tech, who looked at me and shook her head.

"She's gone," she told me in a low, quiet voice.

. . .

We went back to our empty, quiet apartment. Her leash was on the counter. Her water bowl was full.

The vet had euthanized her as soon as they knew we were on our way.

"I couldn't let you see that," she told me. "There was a lot of blood. It was coming from everywhere, you wouldn't have wanted to see that."

The blood didn't matter. It wouldn't have mattered. She was just a little dog. And she died alone, scared, shaking, and without us.

I felt like someone had peeled my skin off. The sting was so constant and raw. When I looked at my husband, I knew he felt the same way.

. . .

Three weeks earlier, we had packed up our house and moved across the country. I took a picture of my husband and Bella in the living room of the house we left. In the picture, her coat is shiny and she is smiling, because I do believe that dogs can smile. She sat in between us for fifteen hundred miles and the three days it took to get to our new town. And for three weeks, we went on walks in our new home, exploring the streets and neighborhoods together. She already had a favorite fir tree on Eleventh Avenue that she liked to visit, and she was starting to get the lay of the land, remembering smells, places, and sounds, getting to know the park.

A week after Bella died, Dr. Greer called us with some test results he had ordered from the emergency clinic. He told me that she had died of autoimmune hemolytic anemia, and that anything she was allergic to could have triggered it. A new smell, a new food, a new plant. It could have been anything, he added; we'll never know exactly what it was. The desert is strikingly different from a rain forest; there were countless new things she had encountered over her last three weeks.

In our empty, quiet apartment, I knew as I put on my walking shoes that if I didn't go back out to Eleventh Avenue and pass that fir tree and go to the park, I wasn't sure I'd be able to for a long time. And that if I didn't, every time I passed one of the streets that we had walked down, I'd resent this new town more and more until I began to hate it.

I went on that walk every day by myself, as the mornings got colder and the leaves began to turn and drop. I bought an iPod because I couldn't handle the silence of not saying "left," "right," "forward," and "down," words that had become so automatic with our walks that I just expected to hear them. I took the same path again and again, morning after morning, until I passed that fir tree and my eyes didn't burn as bitterly, and I could walk by the park without my throat swelling up quite as tightly.

And then, one day, I had just left the park and was walking back to the apartment when a girl walking in front of me turned left. I turned left, too, even though I needed to go straight. She walked for two blocks and then turned right, so I walked for two blocks and turned right. I quickened my pace to try and catch up with her. When she began to turn in to a driveway, I started to run. I had done this before. Not to her, not to the same girl, but to other people, but I had never gone this far. I was stalking her, and I could not let her get into the house at the end of that driveway.

"Excuse me!" I called out to her as I waved my arm. "Excuse me!"

She turned and looked at me, and I could tell she was confused as I came closer.

"I'm sorry," I said as I laughed a little and tried to catch my breath. "But I lost . . . it was sudden, we lost . . . I . . . I was wondering . . . Can I . . . pet your dog?"

She looked at me oddly, as if she wasn't sure whether she should come closer or run away screaming.

"Please?" I said, smiling a little and still breathing heavily; my voice cracked.

"Okay," she said as she nodded and warily came closer, bringing her golden retriever with her.

I scratched the dog on its ears, and I rubbed its head. "You're so pretty," I said to it.

The dog was very nice and let me pet it some more. When it looked at me, it was smiling.

"I'm sorry," I apologized to the girl, who had stood there not saying anything. "I don't mean to be weird. This is so weird. I'm really sorry."

"You lost your dog?" she asked me.

I nodded and smiled firmly with my lips closed.

"I miss her," I said finally, and petted the retriever on the head one more time, and then I thanked the girl.

I turned around and went home, back to the apartment, that quiet, quiet apartment, and when I got there, I already knew that I was never going to walk that way again.

• • •

In February we finally found a little house in a wonderful neighborhood that even had a park without one single tweaker, a Good Morning Tranny grilling her bacon steak at dawn, or a gang of homies dominating the picnic tables. Kids played baseball and soccer at this park, and the swing set actually still had swings. We moved in at the end of March, just in time for spring.

And puppies.

I wasted no time scouring Petfinder.com, the local no-kill shelter, and the county pound. I found Rosie, a seven-month-old German shepherd that had just passed her Canine Good Citizen's test and was trained by a convicted juvenile offender as a part of his rehabilitation.

"She's adorable," I said to my husband as I pointed to her picture on the computer screen, showing one floppy ear.

"No," he said flatly. "I don't think we're ready. I know I won't be ready at least until this semester is over."

A month later I found Snowball, an Alaskan malamute who was completely blind in one eye, partially deaf, and being fostered in Tacoma.

"We will talk about this when the semester ends," my husband reminded me. "In the meantime, please stop looking at those websites. I don't like saying no to you all the time, and every time

I do, it breaks your heart. We are not ready for a dog. I am not ready for a dog, plus we have a nineteen-year-old cat with shabby kidneys. Something that big and white would look like a polar bear to him. And we need a dog that likes cats."

I wasn't trying to replace Bella, and we both knew that. But at the same time, I hated the quiet. I wanted to hear the tinkling of tags and the *bump-bump-bump-bump-bump* behind me when someone with a wagging tail dropped a ball, signaling that playtime needed to commence and quickly.

I wanted a friend.

The morning that my husband was to take his last final exam of the semester, I logged onto the website for the county pound. And there, halfway down the list of dogs available for adoption, was a picture of four little puppies.

"Well, there you are," I said to the little blond baby with her head down, the only one whose face I couldn't see.

"Today is your last final, right?" I called to my husband, who was putting his coat on in the next room.

"Yup," he said.

"Hurry home right after you're finished taking the test," I advised.

"Oooh, why?" he asked as he grabbed his book bag. "Are you planning a surprise?"

"Not really," I said, and then pointed to the screen. "We have to go and get her. That one."

And it was fine if my husband wanted to talk about it after the test was over. That was okay. We had plenty of time to talk about if getting a dog was the right thing for us as we were driving over there to pick her up.

When my husband came home, he put down his book bag and I picked up my car keys.

"We'll do the 'good dog' test," I told him. "We'll test her temperament, and if she's a wild beast, if she's aggressive, if she shows dominant signs, we won't bring her home. How's that?"

"I need a promise from you," my husband said, looking simply defeated.

"I'm promising," I said as we pulled out of the driveway and into the street.

And the moment I opened the front door to the pound, I saw her, being cuddled by the lady at the front desk.

"Can I help you?" said a woman sitting next to her.

"I'm here for her," I said, pointing at the little blond-and-white puppy, who, when she looked at me, revealed her one pony-brown and one sparkling blue eye, both rimmed in black, like Maybelline eyeliner.

From behind me, my husband let out a gasp as if he'd been punched in the gut.

"She's the last one left of that litter, and we never get puppies in here," the lady who was holding her said as she came around and handed me the four-pound, cream-and-white-colored Australian shepherd mix puppy, which I then promptly handed over to my husband and watched him begin to melt like a Milky Way in the sun.

She was our girl, and by the time his hands wrapped around her little chest to hold her for the first time, he was ready for a dog.

The Extended Warranty, the Extended Waistband, and the Repairman Who Almost Became a Hostage

Suddenly, my treadmill came to a halt.

It didn't let out an aching, tired groan, it didn't shrilly emit a gasping, high-pitched shriek, it just stopped. Without much fanfare or struggle, it simply ceased operations and slowly exhaled its last breath in a near-silent *poof*.

Unbelievably, I was on it when it lapsed into the deepest of comas as it slowly rolled to a complete halt and then turned quiet. I attacked the control panel with my fingers, pushing this button and that button, then pushing them harder so the treadmill understood that I meant business, but I couldn't get any life signals on it at all. It wouldn't beep, wouldn't turn on; the console and the display were dead. Nothing. There was just horrible, complete silence.

That is, until I jumped off the treadmill and gave out a whoop worthy of a hillbilly trapping a possum, because, in that moment of sudden silence, my dream had amazingly come true. It was the day I had been waiting for, the day that my investment would pay off, and it had been five years in the making, even if the timing was a little bad. In three months, I would be going on a book tour, and I wanted to lose a good thirty pounds. Because honestly, the ass had to go. It *had to go.* Man, I knew it was out of hand when I completely outgrew the size selection at Banana Republic, but I tried to tell myself they were just cutting corners and outsourcing their sizing to Caracas, where the people are much smaller and eat more fruit. Then I was at the mall when I saw a portly girl with an enormous butt in a green jacket strutting down the walkway like she was something else—really, she looked like a giant avocado. Then as she got closer, her eyes met mine. She gave me the same dirty look I gave her, and then we both gasped in horror as we realized we were both looking into the mirror. And not a metaphorical one, either. I had experienced the Awful Glimpse— a sudden and unexpected look at yourself in which you have no preparation, no warning, and no time to hide behind a couch or landmass. It is gruesome. The Awful Glimpse is an unforgiving, unfiltered portrait of the real you when you least expect it.

So in light of that nightmare, this dead treadmill was my reverie, full and bountiful and golden, come to fruition to pay me handsomely for five years of patience and five hundred dollars' worth of Sears fitness equipment warranties.

Now, I know you think I'm a sucker for actually buying the extended warranty, and the fact of the matter is that I am. Nobody buys the extended warranties unless they've also just transferred some money into the bank account of the prince of Nigeria or, like my mother, are currently a member of the Decorative Spatula of the Month Club and have, at their disposal, spatulas for any given holiday, plus auxiliary spatulas with delightful images of things like flip-flops, bumblebees, or cartoon characters on them. The sorts of things you'd envision while looking at a regular, naked spatula, thinking, My God, you'd be exquisite if you only had an image of a delicately striped candy cane embedded in your transparent, lithe little body!

Nobody.

But I bought the extended warranty, along with the likes of the meek who are afraid to disappoint the salesperson if they say no, the people who put more than a buck in the church basket on Sunday, and the spookers who start buying extra canned food every time they hear the words "bird flu." These are the people who buy extended warranties, and although it's true that I have a secret compartment in my closet that hides two cases of Dinty Moore beef stew in case a ravenous, surly mob invades my house after society has collapsed due to one of a variety of events, I did not buy the extended warranty because I was a sucker necessarily, but because I'm *me*. I have years of purchasing experience with myself, and I knew that when the timer tick-tocked on the very second after the manufacturer's ninety-day warranty was up, I would somehow spill a two-liter bottle of Pepsi all over the console or a chunk of Milky Way Midnight bar would fall out of my mouth and work its way into the wheels of the conveyor belt. I'm no fool. Ninety days after I refused the extended warranty and brought my new microwave home, the plastic ceiling dripped all over my last bag of Extreme Psycho Butter microwave popcorn like alien guts and charged toward the finale by bursting into flame, taking the popcorn with it. Three months after I unpacked my new vacuum cleaner, it suffered a stroke after ingesting a particularly girthy hairball and a nickel that took me five tries of rolling over it before my new vacuum would even suck them up. And then there was the twenty-one-inch television that was purchased after my six-month-old, mere infant TV/DVD combo went on strike, and held disc two of *Gilmore Girls, Second Season* hostage, which despite attempted surgery with a fork and a wad of chewing gum was never recovered. The twenty-one-inch TV never even survived its toddlerhood, as a year into its life it simply stopped responding, and, extended-warranty-less, I wrapped up the cord and talked a friend of mine with an electronically handy husband into taking it. Despite my better judgment, I allowed her to plug it in before carting it away, and within a mere moment of turning it on, a full-color picture bloomed onto the screen, as Lorelai and Rory sipped their twelfth coffee in as many scenes, roll-eyed each other in delightful banter, and basked in the glory that is being a size double zero tagteam. My friend was delighted and waved "thank you" from her car before driving away with the free television in her backseat that had not been defective after all but merely unplugged.

And even though an extended warranty doesn't cover electronics not working because your U-boat feet have repeatedly kicked the plug from its union with the socket, the extended-warranty people could have told me that and then mocked me, respectively, which would have cost me far less than the resulting sixty-nine dollars for a new TV and sixty-nine dollars for the ensuing extended warranty.

And the truth of the matter is that my treadmill breaks. Quite often. It has broken at least once a year since I bought it, therefore, I've just about broken even or may even be a little ahead of the extended-warranty game, and once a year, some very nice lady from India will call me and remind me of that, right before I give her my Sears credit card number to renew my sucker status.

"Thank you very much, Miss Laurie Notaro," she says.

"I *love* papadum," I gush.

Whenever the treadmill broke, I shut the thing off and called the lady in India, who called the repair person to come and fix it, and in each case, they showed up within their designated forty-eight-hour appointment window with their toolboxes and their treadmill wisdom and greeted me with a smile and a handshake—with one exception.

Her name was Maria, and she had been fixing my treadmill for three years in a row when I felt the machine shudder and shake and I knew it was time to make the call. I made an appointment for later that week, but the day before she was to come, Maria called and said she couldn't make it because she had a bad cold, so was Monday okay? I agreed, happy that I could sleep in, and I did exactly that. Due to my sleep mask and earplugs and blessed be thy Tylenol PM, it was a long, luxurious sleep. When I rose, my husband was already up, judging by the empty side of the bed, so I got up, found my big, fuzzy slippers (which completed my bold ensemble of a white pair of grandma panties and a *far* too tight tank top), and shuffled down the hall past my office and past the living room to the bathroom to get my morning business started.

And a grand morning it was, with a hearty business agenda to attend to, and I called the meeting to order. As my morning thunder rumbled and my colon went bowlin', my husband suddenly appeared in the doorway of the bathroom.

He looked angry, very angry. "What are you doing?" I sort of figured he was saying, since I still had my earplugs in and couldn't hear a thing.

I winced and got a little offended myself. I mean, *come on,* it was *morning.* Things needed to be attended to, like my morning symphony. I didn't bother him while *he* was having his morning time!

"Oh, sure," I said as I waved him away with my hand. "It's not like this is something you haven't seen before!"

"SHUT THAT DOOR!" he seemed to be yelling, and his brow was furrowing deeper.

"Oh, for Christ's sake, lay off, would you?" I replied, starting to get angry at his suddenly offended demeanor. "We had Mexican last night! I'm sure your potty activities weren't all that dainty, either!"

At that point, he began to get very animated and pretended to shut an imaginary door, and was saying things that I could neither read on his lips nor even hear. And damned if I was taking my earplugs out. I liked the muffled, droning silence of my private universe, and I was going to enjoy it for as long as I could. If he was going to play Miss Priss, that was his problem. I looked at him, furrowed my brow, and shook my head, and very quickly he appeared to become outraged. Frankly, I couldn't figure it out. All of a sudden, after how many years of being married to me, and *now* he's upset that all semblance of propriety and decorum had faded away and crumbled after our third date? If he had always been appalled at my open-door policy, why not say something to begin with? Why let it fester for years and years and years until it spurred a reaction such as this, leaving him angry and myself embarrassed? Not to mention that I'm not the only one in the house with that policy, thank you very much. So why pick on me, in the morning when I'm still groggy, quite deaf, and so full of bean-and-cheese-burrito by-products that if I was to come into contact with a heat source, I'd go up like the *Hindenburg*?

"Whatever," I said as I expended a little extra effort, even squeezed my eyes shut, and delivered something I knew was spectacular. "*That* one's for you, weirdo!"

The horror that attacked my husband's face was simply unparalleled. He shook his head, and with his hands balled up into little fists, he began marching in place like a little soldier.

I shrugged and threw my hands up in the air. I had no idea what he was doing.

"Are you calling me a bathroom Nazi?" I queried, and got no response.

Then he pretended to be carrying a bag, proceeded to "open" the bag, took some pretend stuff out, and then embarked on what looked like knitting. This was even more insane than his previous antics.

"You want me to make you a hat?" I asked. "A soldier hat? *Now?* You want me to make it *now?* Did you eat something that didn't smell quite right from the fridge or take the dog's arthritis pill instead of your multivitamin?"

Suddenly, my husband stopped marching and began furiously pointing toward my office. Then he marched again. Then he opened his pretend bag and returned to his mime knitting.

In my office, I began to piece together, is a knitting Nazi. No.

In my office is a walking knitter. No. In my office, I can walk and knit.

"In my office, I can walk on my treadmill and knit?" I guessed, to which my husband shook his head and began pretend hammering.

In my office, I can walk on the treadmill and build things? I can walk on the treadmill and work with tools? Work with tools? Using tools on the treadmill? Fix things on the treadmill? Fixing the treadmill with tools the broken treadmill awwww holy shit in my office is being fixed by a repairperson with tools while I've been performing my best trumpet imitation on the crapper with the door open half naked not to mention I just walked down the hallway with nothing on but a tank top, slippers, and my grandma panties holy shit good God holy shit!

If there were an Olympic event for mortified half-naked women to jump off of a toilet and slam a bathroom door shut with the might of a hurricane, I would have at least won a bronze.

At least.

Oh no, I thought. She heard everything! Maria heard everything, and even *I* didn't hear everything. I can't come out now. I'm going to have to stay in the bathroom until she leaves.

And then I heard a muffled, tiny *knock knock knock* on the door before it opened and my husband stuck his head in.

"Why didn't you shut the door when I told you to?" he hissed at me in a harsh whisper.

"I didn't know what you were talking about!" I shot back.

"I can't believe you were prancing and farting around with someone else here like you didn't even care!" he continued.

"Maria canceled her appointment! She's not supposed to be

here until Monday!" I replied. "How was I supposed to know she came anyway?"

"I tried to tell you," my husband answered. "It's not her! They sent another lady! You just kept sitting there, making those . . . sounds! And you didn't stop! You just wouldn't stop!"

"I couldn't hear you from over there!" I hurled back. "I have my earplugs in!"

"TAKE," he said as he raised his hands, "THOSE," put them close to my face, "THINGS," stuck his left hand in my right ear and plucked out a conical piece of yellow foam, "OUT!" and did the same with my left ear. "Now will you please cover yourself?" he begged, and I heard that loud and clear.

"Sure," I said spitefully. "I have a shower cap and a washcloth. Which would you prefer?"

"I'll go get your robe," he said, exasperated, but it didn't matter. There was no way I was coming out of the bathroom, even if the repair lady decided she was going to build me a whole new treadmill and it took days. Surely, she knew I was in there, and I knew I was in there, but never would the two of us meet. I had my husband bring me a can of Diet Pepsi and a Pop-Tart. I hung out in the bathtub for quite a while until I heard her toolbox shut, the front door close, and her truck rev its engine and then pull away.

Needless to say, I am especially careful about scheduling any morning appointments, lest my methane version of *The Ride of the Valkyries* makes a redux while a repairperson is quietly lurking around my house after I've drugged myself up with over-the-counter sedatives.

So this time, after the treadmill ground to a halt and my whooping and hollering was all done, when time to call the lady in

India came, I made an afternoon appointment, and I couldn't wait. You see, I've heard that treadmill wheeze, I've watched as the walking belt was severed, I've felt it jolt and shake. But this time it was different. It had never simply just stopped before, unable to be revived by putting the plug back in the socket or rebooting the console. Nope. This time, I knew it was gone for good, I had finally worked it to death, and that meant only one thing.

If it couldn't be fixed, then a new one, a brand-new treadmill, would be delivered to my doorstep as a reward for paying one hundred dollars a year for half a decade.

I wanted the new treadmill. And not only would it be a new treadmill, it would be the new model. Have you seen them? They have built-in fans and cup holders and fluffy shock absorbers that make climbing at a 6 percent incline like walking up the cottony steps of Heaven. Some even have snack stations where your Oreos can wait until you devour them like a caveman in your primal sweat as an "I burned sixty calories!" reward. I wanted one of those, one of the treadmills that all you have to do is stand on them and your chunkosity melts away. So when I called Sears to claim my prize of a new treadmill, they told me a technician would come out to repair the problem—in four weeks. *Four weeks.* By then, I assumed, I would have gained enough weight to grow out of my big girl clothes and come home one day to find my living room full of strangers holding duffel bags as my husband explained, "You don't have any friends here or people who like you, so I paid people standing at the bus station five dollars each to be here. This is your Fat Intervention."

"That's in a month!" I cried to the operator.

"A month is not four weeks, ma'am," the operator scolded me.

Four weeks. I looked at my old, dusty treadmill, sighed, and agreed.

I could wait for four weeks for a new treadmill. Four weeks and a brand-new one, with built-in fans and the Stairway to Heaven belt, would be in its place.

I waited patiently during those weeks. I gained weight and went up a size. Had to buy new pants. Had to buy two pairs of new pants. Had to buy a skirt. And three shirts. Getting fatter. Waiting for the treadmill. Watchin' lots of TV. Started using safety pins to keep my shirts closed. "How fat do you plan on getting?" the worry in my husband's eyes said to me. "Have you seen your ass? I looked at it last night and it looked like two bags of gravel hanging from your waist!"

The days of the calendar finally peeled away to the day of reckoning. The day before, I had started cleaning my office to get the piles of boxes and house overflow off the treadmill where they had accumulated for the past month while my body doubled and dimpled. I cleaned the dust off the treadmill belt, wiped it from the dead, lifeless console.

I detailed that treadmill to show the technician how good I was to it.

It took hours. Milky Ways are hard to scrape up, especially after they've turned white.

Then the phone rang. It was Sears. The technician couldn't make it, so was tomorrow okay? Even though I ground my teeth (which had also gained weight) together, I wanted to appease the technician, to grease the gears, shall we say, and make him or her more disposed to granting me my precious treadmill dream.

Sure, I said, I can wait one more day.

Then the hallowed day arrived. It was yesterday. The technician was supposed to arrive between 1 and 5 P.M.

It was 1:30.

2:30.

3:30.

4:00.

4:15.

4:37.

The phone rang.

"Yep, this is Ted," he said. "So your treadmill is running slow, the report says."

"NO!" I yelped, desperate at the thought that he might not fully comprehend the starkness of the situation. "It's not slow! It's just dead. It stopped when I was on it. And there's been nothing since."

Ted was silent.

"Nothing!" I cried again for emphasis.

"Anything on the console?" Ted asked. "Does it light up, beep, make any noise?"

"No," I replied. "It's just dead."

Ted paused for a minute.

"Do me a favor," he said. "Do you see where the power cord connects to the treadmill?"

"Yes," I said.

"Now, next to it, there's a little switch," he instructed. "Push it twice."

"Okay, hang on," I said with an exaggerated sigh, agitated that I had to crawl onto the treadmill to push a stupid button that I knew wouldn't work. The treadmill was dead. There was no bringing it back. I just wanted him to do his job, get to my house, and give me a new one with the snack station.

I crawled onto the treadmill, found the button, and pushed it. Twice.

Beep. I heard from above me. *Beep.*

"I hear a *beep!*" Ted said. "That'll do you. If it happens again, hit that circuit-breaker switch. I'm gonna get going, I'm running late."

He hung up before I could respond, before I could even say anything. He was just gone; he never even walked inside my house; I never even had a chance to fart him out. I believed my dream was dashed.

But the very next day, as I trudged along, a spark of hope renewed my big, fancy plan.

I smelled smoke. Then I *saw* smoke, and as if I needed an excuse to jump off the treadmill, I did just that, my hop followed by a jig of happiness. This was not something pushing a little button would fix. This was *smoke.* That meant a burning *something.* So I called the lady in India. In four weeks, she said, someone would come to my house and fix it.

Four weeks later, a new guy named Chris showed up, and by this time, I was wearing my husband's T-shirts and sweatpants and had even become too fat for my own shoes. He looked at the treadmill, which I had now begun calling the Dreadmill, assessed its damage, nodded when I said, "Do you see it smoking?" and said that he'd need to order the part from Portland because Sears didn't let him carry parts on his truck anymore.

"Are you sure you just need a part?" I asked carefully. "Because that, right there, is smoke. Maybe it's better if we don't take our chances, you know? Can't you just total it out, because if my car was on fire, I think State Farm would call that a total."

"I think all we need is a new motor," Chris said cheerfully. "That should fix the problem." Then he said he'd be back in one week, which was fine. From my waistband, I heard some elastic pop.

The following Friday, Chris showed up with a new motor, just like he said he would, and put it in, just as he said he would, and then ran the Dreadmill, which within seconds flat began emitting smoke.

"See, I'm thinking I could cook a hot dog under there," I pointed out. "Will you total it out now?"

"Hmmm," Chris said, pondering his obvious miscalculation and diagnosis. "Oh, no, that's another part. I thought it was the motor, but I ordered the wrong thing."

Now I tried to calm myself, because at this point, I could clearly see that I was not getting the snack-station Dream Barbie Treadmill, I was going to be stuck with my same of piece-of-shit, breaking-down-every-year Dreadmill, and not only was I stuck with it, but in the last two and a half months it hadn't worked at all and the immediate future wasn't appearing too bright, either.

And I was still paying for the extended warranty.

So I gathered myself together and asked if he had a part on the truck.

He mentioned that he used to carry those parts, but gave me the same line about getting them from Portland, and it would be another week before it arrived.

Now, to be very, very truthful, I tried so hard to keep myself together, I really, really did, but I felt my eyes get all hot and watery, and so I looked straight at him for a couple of seconds and it was evident to me that I was on the verge of having a full-on emotional meltdown, complete with tears, blubbering, and possible drool.

So I just said to him, "I have to ask you to leave. You have to go, because I am going to start crying and I don't want you to see me cry."

And he got really flustered and didn't know what to do. I think the only thing that could have made him more nervous is if I had uttered the word "hostage." He just kept apologizing over and over again. "I'm sorry, I didn't know it was that part, I'm sorry, I'm sorry. I'll be back as soon as I can, maybe next Friday," which was, indeed, in exactly a week.

And that, as it turns out, was the pin in my grenade. That was all it took. I looked at him again, and this time, I looked hard right at him, and said almost quietly, "Do you see how fat I am? Do you see how FAT I AM? I have ONE pair of pants that fits me and this treadmill has now been broken for almost three months. I have four weeks to lose thirty pounds so I can fit into something to go on this book tour. I had three months before; now I have FOUR WEEKS!" Then my voice cracked. "People are going to see me fat! Would you like it if people saw you fat?"

And then, as Chris was scurrying to his van, his fingers clutched tight around his toolbox, doubtful to ever return, I realized that indeed, there might have been one thing that was worse than farting out a symphony within earshot of an unsuspecting treadmill repairperson.

A Kung Fu Person, a Tollbooth, and a Swinging Bridge in Less Than Twenty-four Hours

"You didn't say *we had to stay,"* my husband said out of the corner of his mouth as we stood in the entrance to the doggie day-care center. "I thought you said we were dropping her off. I would have never come if I knew you were dragging me to a little dog's birthday party."

"I didn't know, either," I said from behind my teeth, which were shown in a wide, big, fake smile. "I thought we just dropped her off and picked her up. Like kids."

"We had to bring a present, like kids," my husband added.

"Maybe we can tie our kid to something, slip away, then come back in an hour," I suggested, still smiling broadly.

"If you make me go to a dog's birthday party, I will never forgive you, and after you die, I will marry the first blonde I meet in an act of retaliatory revenge," he cautioned.

"Big deal," I shot back. "I was planning on haunting the shit out of you, anyway. A blonde sleeping in my bed and drinking out of my Bigfoot mug will make it all that more rich and rewarding when I hover over her at night and freeze her with supernatural terror."

"Well, look who's here!" Mandie, the proprietor of the day-care center, said when she saw the three of us huddled. "You're just in time for Lola Chanel's birthday party!"

All right, go ahead and say it. Just say it. I'm an asshole for taking my dog to a birthday party, and I know it. I'd be the first one to agree. But when we brought our new puppy home, I knew that I wanted to do things different with her than we did with Bella. As a puppy, Bella didn't encounter too many other dogs because we were terrified to take her on a walk after our elderly neighbor, Mrs. Crowley, described the horror of having an unrestrained dog charge at her and Pinky, her ten-pound poodle concoction, after it decided that Pinky looked like Pup-Peroni and forced the eighty-four-year-old woman to try to fight the predator off with her metal cane, to no avail. And as a result, when we moved into our apartment in Oregon, our silly little blind, unsocialized dog was terrified of every other dog in the building and occasionally challenged them to bring it on, believing with inappropriate fervor that they were trespassing and that what she only could kind of see couldn't hurt her.

Therefore, our new little puppy, who after three days was still unnamed, went for walks twice a day in our nice, new neighborhood, where mean dogs didn't eat little poodle-dos on a Tuesday afternoon while being beaten by a handicapped woman with a piece of medical equipment, where I wouldn't be afraid that the maleficent corgi leader of the dog gang wouldn't try to jump my dog into his "club," and we didn't have to run past the house where four puppies had died in as many years from parvo, although the owners believed the dogs all expired from licking antifreeze rather than from not getting their shots.

But she needed a name, and after my husband shot down my suggestion of Fanny, inspired by the way the puppy exuberantly shook her butt when she wagged her tail, I was fresh out of ideas.

One thing I did know, however, was that I wanted to name her something that I was sure every other dog wouldn't have engraved on a tag around its neck in a year. When we brought Bella home, she was the only Bella we knew of, but by the time she died, every dog I ran into was named Bella. Now, it's not like I invented the name, but it sorta sucks when you think you've found something pretty, nice, and uncommon, then the next thing you know, it's in the top ten, right under Buddy, and you can't say your dog's name in the waiting room at the vet's without six others answering you. Ask any mother of an Ashley what she would do if given the chance again in 1989, and you get the picture. The same thing happened with Chelsea, our mildly retarded black lab, so eventually I just started calling her Chigger to see if anyone wanted to steal that name, too. Not a taker.

So when it came to this puppy, I wanted to make sure she was the only ____ on the block. We went through all of our typical names, but they sounded either too contrived or too pompous. Daisy. Ruby. Aria. Molly. Nothing seemed to fit, not to mention that we weren't even agreeing on the names that didn't work.

"You know, I really don't like Walt Whitman for a girl," I mentioned kindly. "What about Janis?"

"*Please*," my husband jeered. "Why don't we just name her

Obligatory Dead Rock Star and get her hooked on Beggin' Strips before she even loses her puppy teeth? What about Edna?"

"Dear Mr. Poetry Graduate Student, every Edna but the vixen St. Vincent Millay is a hundred pounds overweight and wears nothing but a housedress, socks, and slippers," I ridiculed. "Here's a good one! What about Zelda?"

"Well, that's quite a namesake," he scoffed. "Do you want a manic-depressive dog who goes crazy and dies in a fire? Do you? What about—"

"Once and for all, we are not naming the dog Emily Dickinson, who lived in self-imposed exile for most of her life by not coming out of her room," I insisted. "Or Gertrude Stein, who was chunky and had a bad haircut, or Anne Sexton, who committed suicide wearing a fur coat and holding a tumbler of vodka."

"All right then, I want to name our dog Christiane," he relented. "Amanpour. Christiane Amanpour. Or Sylvia Poggioli."

"You and your foreign-correspondent fetish!" I shot back. "Let's bring it back to America, okay? Anderson Cooper!"

"Kate Winslet," he replied.

"I'd rather eat the dog than name her after your fantasy significant other!" I volleyed. "What about George Clooney?"

"We are not naming our new puppy George Clooney!" he cried. "This is madness. We need to think of a good name and think of one fast. For the past three days we've been calling her Dog Not Bella, and that can't continue. So put on your thinking cap, and let's make a pact that we won't vocalize it until it's something good that can work, okay?"

"Okay," I agreed.

We were quiet for the rest of the night. Every now and then, one of us would lurch forward a tiny bit, open our mouth, think better of it, and sink back into the cushions of the sofa.

We went to bed after putting Dog Not Bella into her crate that sat alongside of us, closed the tiny wire door, and listened to her whimper.

"How long do you think she's going to keep crying like that?" my husband asked.

"I don't know," I said. "This is the first time we've tried to raise a dog the right way, otherwise I'd toss an old pair of my panties in there and we'd be asleep by now."

"I guess we just have to let her cry," my husband murmured. "I guess she has to get used to the crate."

"I know, but it's so hard," I agreed. "She is so adorable, her fluffy cream-colored fur, that speckled little nose, and those huge, huge, HUGE eyes just like Bella's lined in black like Maybelline."

My husband turned toward me and stared.

"Hmmmmm," he said with a smile.

"Hmmmmm," I said right back.

"Well," he finally said. "What do you think?"

"It's better than George Clooney, I admit," I replied. "But all I hear in my head is that Chuck Berry song."

"Yeah," he agreed. "I like that song, but not enough to hear it for the next fifteen years the first time we tell someone her name and they sing it at us."

"Thinking that they're the only one who has ever sung it to us and that it's so clever," I added.

"Do you think Maybelline was Maeby Fünke's full name on my favorite but ill-fated yet critically acclaimed series *Arrested Development*?" I wondered aloud for the sake of any reader who was unaware of the show and thus complicit in its premature death.

"The teenage cousin who pretended to go to high school but lied her way into becoming a movie executive in a single afternoon?" my husband asked. "I don't know. Maybe."

"Maeby," I said with a final nod, and with that, the little dog with the speckled nose and one blue and one brown eye had a name.

. . .

I decided to invest in a behavioral puppy kit and began studying how to raise the best-socialized and well-adjusted dog I possibly could and at the same time, according to the workbook, "not change the dog's personality or natural spunk."

This required a great deal of participation on my part, and I had to be willing to activate my suspension of disbelief, which is sometimes a challenge to turn off, particularly if I'm watching something with Samuel Jackson in it (seriously, the man might really want take a good look at the coiffure requirements of a role before he signs on for his next project, because with every successive movie his wigs get nastier and nastier. I don't see how it can get any worse unless Jackson pops up in his next movie wearing a fright wig or gels all of his hair into one big horn).

For example, as instructed by one of our assignments in the *How to Not Ruin Your Dog and Avoid Lawsuits, Too, Handbook,* I assumed the role of a toddler and rolled around on the ground babbling nonsense and poking at Maeby, gently tugging at her ears, tail, and coat, simultaneously giving her treats so she wouldn't one day bite the face off a baby who most likely wasn't invited to my house in the first place.

But as I got further into the handbook, things became a little more complicated. If I really wanted to socialize my puppy and prepare her for today's urban world, the kit told me, I needed to be fully committed to broadening her horizons as big and wide as possible. And to ensure that I would accomplish all of my objectives, the puppy kit included a checklist of potential Objects of Terror that Maeby needed to encounter and get a treat from before she reached her sixteenth week, which would mark the end of the most crucial socialization and imprinting stage of her life. Looking at the list, I was instantly overwhelmed at the sheer number of targets, which included

- People of different ethnicities (black, white, Asian, Indian, Native American, Latino, and if you could score a primitive jungle person from a tribe in New Guinea, your dog got membership in the UN)

- People in uniform (postal worker, firefighter, police officer, meter reader, telephone worker, ambulance attendant— apparently, the puppy kit had obtained my last blood-pressure reading and foresaw some tragedy in our future)

- Animals (other healthy dogs, hamsters, geese, and goats)

- People holding umbrellas or wearing sunglasses, hats, beards, helmets, punk hairdos, or raincoats, and the bald

- People with canes, legs in casts, metal-frame walkers, wheel-chairs, baby carriages, luggage, erratic body moves, limps, or odd gaits (this is when living in Phoenix could have come in real handy, as most of our neighbors began to bring metal canes, walkers, or bats with them to venture outside after Mrs. Crowley's poodle was turned into a chew toy by a cannibalistic pit bull).

- Environmental hazards and noise pollution: sirens, thunder and lightning, fireworks, the airport, building demolition, loudspeakers, and so on

The list continued for four more pages.

I broke out into a cold sweat. I didn't know how I could possibly pull this off. I looked at Maeby, her adorable speckled nose resting between her two white-sock paws as she slept on a pile of my dirty underwear in the laundry room, and I thought, "How I have failed you already. You never had a chance when you came to this house. I might as well have locked you in a cage and thrown a black sheet over it. You poor, feral, frightened creature. I should have named you Sybil with all the damage I'm about to do to you!"

But then I had an idea. If I could combine these Objects of Terror, there was a real possibility that I could expose Maeby to all of them before her imprint-expiration date. After all, this was Eugene, bastion of everything odd, unlikely, and—as much as those in the Pacific Northwest want to argue the point, *unnatural*. During our first week here, for example, my husband saw a family bicycling down the street, each member dressed consistently in homemade, brightly colored knitwear made of yarn most likely spun from the fur of the animals living with them. The mom had an accordion balanced on her handlebars, the dad, typically identified as such by unruly facial hair and a "'Twas the Night Before Christmas" stocking cap, had a fiddle, and the little girl had a birdcage with a chicken it. Had I encountered them at the right time, I could have crossed about fifteen Objects of Terror Targets off our list. It would have saved me the equivalent of an entire day had I otherwise searched for all of those individual attributes one at a time.

I imagined her socialization period ending like the closing of a garage door, rolling down slowly, slowly, slowly, and in the final seconds hearing a disembodied voice proclaim, ". . . and your time . . . is . . . UP!" as the door hits the ground with a hollow, metal crash, and all of our future opportunities of getting a treat from a Filipino skateboarder wearing a witch hat and a raincoat while shooting off fireworks being gone forever.

"All right," I said to my husband during Maeby's fifteenth week as I rolled out the spreadsheet on the dining room table. "We still have a lot of incompletes here. She still needs to go to a rally or protest, and there's a sit-in tomorrow at city hall, at which, if we play our cards right, we can knock out Hacky Sackers, a drum circle, a juggler, and if we're lucky and things get out of hand, some cops. It's a fiver, got it? This one's important. Keep an eye out for a Rastafarian and someone from Vietnam, because we've got some ground to cover there, too."

"Got it," my husband said. "What's the protest for?"

"The right to breast-feed in the food court at the mall without the use of a covering blanket," I replied.

"Ooooh, that's a good one," he said with a smile.

"I thought you'd like it," I said.

"No, I mean, we can also knock out infants, toddlers, strollers, and flapjack hippie boobs," he said, pointing to each correlating category on the chart.

"Flapjack hippie boobs aren't on here," I said, laughing.

"They should be," he opined. "They are far more frightening than most of the things on this list. It's a good thing hippies don't wear shoes, otherwise some of those women would get their boobs tangled in their laces."

"Now, I need you to bring her back here by five because she has to see rush hour," I reminded him. "And you still haven't brought home a kite."

"I haven't had time!" he whined. "On Saturday she went to the rodeo, on Sunday I spent four hours looking for a tobogganist, although I did find some kayakers, and last night we went to that Republican fund-raiser to expose her to drunk people and strong scents."

"You know, I don't want to hear it," I snipped. "If you want a dog that is tormented every time she sees a kite because someone was too busy to stop into Target for five seconds, then you're the one who has to live with that, not me. How would you like to spend your whole life thinking a kite is going to swoop down and eat you with a big dowel-and-nylon mouth?"

"Come on," he replied, obviously defensive. "Who was the one who got 'spectators at a 10K'? I did! I did! That was me! I also got 'people swimming' and took her to the tarmac!"

"That wasn't 'people swimming,' it was *a Jacuzzi*," I reminded him. "Which *isn't even on the list*. And on the tarmac, you couldn't even get out of the car. The kit said 'not on a hot day,' but you decided to take her on a 'hot day.' Now I have to wait for some clouds to roll in so I can bring her back! And I already did 'drunk people' the night you finished off that wine by yourself."

"That's it," he said, throwing his hands up. "I don't have to take this! I'm leaving!"

"Where are you going?" I demanded.

"Where do you think? I'm taking Maeby to 'an active railway,'" he shot back.

"Now?" I questioned. "I was going to shoot her with the hair dryer!"

"I'll knock out a homeless person, too, okay?" he said, then turned around and pointed his finger toward me. "But I am *not* doing '*hot-air balloon.*'"

I pursed my lips and shook my head, glaring at him. "You know I'm afraid of heights," I hissed. "You always knew I couldn't do 'hot-air balloon'!"

"Then that's something *you* have to live with," my husband concluded.

"Try to walk her over a manhole cover and a grate!" I shouted after him after he picked up the puppy and headed for the door. "And we're still missing 'speed walkers'!"

"Oh, God," I said to myself as I turned and rubbed my hand over my chin, looking over all of the empty spots still covering the chart. "Where am I going to find a kung fu person, a tollbooth, and a swinging bridge in less than twenty-four hours?"

When time was up, it was up. Our window had closed and was now bolted shut. We did the best that we could, and although, with a helping hand from Lady Luck, we were able cover "cars backfiring," "beach party/bonfires," and "hammocks," I can admit with a regrettable sense of failure that if Maeby ever encounters a Native American mime involved in any sort of building demolition, I simply cannot predict what she will do.

• • •

After Maeby's socialization was complete, we both thought that puppy obedience training should be next on the list, so I opened the phone book. The next thing I knew, I was driving along a country road deep in the forest somewhere with my puppy sitting between my husband and me, all of us wondering where the road was taking us.

And in about twenty minutes, we rolled up to a house in the middle of nowhere. A large woman in sweatpants and sweatshirt opened the door, her hair in a ponytail, her face entirely unamused.

After I introduced the three of us, she stepped aside to let us in, and an unidentified and concentrated smell hit us from all angles. "I know that smell," I said to myself as I took another whiff of the offensive odor. "I know it. Where is it from? Oh yes. Yes, I know. It smells like zebras. Zebras and elephants and lions, the odors and aromas of Africa. Yet, I have never been to Africa, though I *have* been to the zoo, and in close proximity to the places where all of those animals go potty. And that is the part of Africa that I am smelling right now. The potty part." Then I spotted the hall and saw that, oddly enough, the top half of the wall was white but the remaining bottom third was a blackish brown. Exactly at dog height.

Holy God, I thought to myself as I tried to resist the compelling urge to swoop Maeby off the ground and away from whatever disease and pestilence was living in that carpet. I've only seen houses like this on *COPS* or *Animal Planet* when people from the ASPCA come out to rescue millions of cats from the clutches of a seventy-three-year-old lady and her mentally stunted son. Even I don't live like this, and before I got married, I almost needed an archeologist to come out and identify some things I hadn't seen for a while that had been hidden under layers and layers of mess.

My husband and I looked at each other intently, as I'm sure we both realized how foolish it was for us, as a couple, to not have invested the time and effort into learning Morse code so that one day we could send secret messages back and forth to each other through eyeblinks and nostril inflation while trapped in the filthiest house on the planet, trying desperately to formulate a plan of escape with our baby dog.

When the sweatpants dog trainer went into the kitchen to fetch her paperwork, we had very little time to coordinate something acute and tricky to secure our release. But there were more important things to be discussed first.

"Look at that wall," I whispered, nodding in that direction. "It's all gross from dogs rubbing against it!"

"That's not dirt," my husband whispered back. "That's from a dog in heat."

Without hesitation, I picked Maeby up off the floor even though I was sure the carpet was doing wonders to boost her immune system, including exposing her to diseases that had been thought long eradicated.

"If she can't teach her dog not to rub its coochie on the wall, how is she going to train Maeby to sit?" I whispered just as the trainer walked back into the room.

I looked her square in the eye.

"I forgot the money," I said simply before we headed out the door.

• • •

Free from the obligation to return to the House of Bitch Blood for further "training," we enrolled Maeby in puppy classes where certainly, dogs had peed, but there were minimum-wage workers to clean it up: at the clean, well-lit, concrete-floored PetSmart.

Which was great, and Maeby did very well with her trainer, Shari, learning to sit, lie down, drop things, to not eat until I gave the word, to heel, and all kinds of other stuff. The only thing the training was lacking, however, was playing with other dogs, and it was really important to me that in five years' time, I didn't wake up one day to a dog who believed she was the boss of everybody and was more than anxious to prove it.

I wanted a dog who played nicely with others, and if I couldn't get that at puppy class, I needed to get it from some-where. One ill-fated afternoon, we set out for our nearby dog park, and the moment I let Maeby off leash, a smarmy, tiny dog with Ernest Borgnine eyes sidled up to Maeby quickly, then jumped on her and began to do his nasty on her leg, even though he only reached midflank on the puppy, even in midthrust.

"Is anyone missing John Holmes?" I joked, thinking it was funny, and looked down to see Maeby looking back toward the dog, her eyes wide with fear. And then I remembered.

She's a baby. She has no idea of what's going on; this *is* her first time at the rodeo!

"You dirty uncle!" I hissed at the little dog, who showed no

signs of stopping, even though he was too tiny to even be touching anything.

I tried to push him away, but he just turned and growled at
me, looking much like a mouse might if it bared its teeth.

"Get off of her, you pedophile! Go chase an ice cream truck
somewhere! She's an infant!" I demanded, trying to move him off
with the toe of my boot. "It shouldn't hurt to be a puppy!"

I called out for someone—anyone—to come and get him, but
no one stepped forth.

"You are lucky her sixteen-week window is already closed, you
little shit, or I'd sue your little doggie balls off," I hissed as I tried
to push him off again.

It was useless. He would not leave her alone. Apparently, this
was a once-in-a-lifetime chance for him, finally finding some
fresh meat at the dog park that wasn't wise to his greasy, preda-
tory ways and couldn't whack him out of the way with the swish of
a fluffy tail.

"All right, that's it," I said, hooking Mae's collar back up to her
leash. "I used to live mere houses away from a real rapist, and if
you really want to play this little game, it is on, Mr. Winkle! I still
have the pepper spray on my key chain!"

I tugged on Maeby's leash and we were off.

"Run, Maeby, run!"

I knew that little son of a bitch couldn't keep up with us with
his tiny toothpick legs, but he gave it the attempt of a lifetime,
chasing us all the way to the fence and going in for one last lurch
before Maeby made a final escape and I shut the gate right behind us.

He stood sorrowfully on the other side of the chain-link fence, still staring at us and barking that his young, nubile harem girl had gotten away.

"You're an asshole!" I said harshly as I pointed at him, and then I looked up at the whole dog park. "This little dog is an asshole! And so is the asshole that owns him!"

Thus, our day at the dog park ended with me tearing out of the parking lot, but not before I flashed my personal sized can of Mace at a two-pound dog who was still standing at the fence, watching us drive away.

• • •

"**That is ridiculous,**" my mother said on the other end of the phone. "A day care for dogs? Why does she have to go to day care? Why did you get a dog if you didn't want her to be home? And why does she have a last initial? Is she like Eman M.?"

"I told you before," I said with a sigh. "Her name is not May B. It's Maeby. One word, no initial."

"Maybe? Like *perhaps*?" she asked. "That's a stupid thing to call a dog."

"I know it is, Mom," I said. "I named her Maeby just so I could hear you say that."

"I know you did," my mother replied. "And you called me just to aggravate me about this moronic dog school. This is what I don't understand: Dogs should be home all day, lying on the floor, not in a big yard running and playing with other dogs, right? Right? Am I right? That's ridiculous. Since when do dogs even want to play with other dogs?"

"Um, I don't know. Since they formed a subspecies of wolf.

Fifteen thousand years ago, or some people say a hundred fifty thousand years," I answered.

"Oh, *come on*," she scoffed. "That's stupid! A hundred fifty thousand years? Who was around then to write that down? You don't know that!"

"Okay," I relented. "Tuesday. The vote was Tuesday. Didn't your dog vote? My dog voted. She even got a sticker that said 'I voted today to play.' It passed by a landslide, although the exit polls in Ohio were a bit iffy."

"I can't believe you pay to take her to a place where she can run around," she went on. "It sounds like a waste of money to me. You could get a good meal for what you pay. Is that what all you tree huggers do all day in Oregon? Take all of your pets to different day-care places? If you had a fish, would it go to fishy day care? Is that what you like to do, living up in your trailer in the woods?"

"I happen to live on a very nice street of well-preserved historic houses," I reminded her. "Where the trees form a canopy over the street in the spring. I have three professors, a librarian, a retired diplomat, and a psychiatrist for neighbors. I do not live in a trailer in the woods, Mom."

"Well," she began, "that's what I tell people so I can hear you say that."

"Oh, hang on," I said. "Maeby wants to talk to Grandma! Say 'Hi, Grandma!'"

"Oh, no! No no no! Don't you pu—"

And then I fumbled with the phone a bit, panted into the receiver, then hung it up.

. . .

And Maeby loved day care. She loooooved it. She made friends immediately, and got report cards at the end of every day detailing what she did, and in Maeby's own voice, leaving comments such as:

"I flirted with Samson a bit, but he's not up to par intellectually for me."

"I made a new friend, Nancy. She steals balls and brings them to me."

"I was voted the 'Marilyn Monroe' of the dogs—beautiful and deeper than anyone knows!"

You know, a chunk of questionable sirloin drenched in Alfredo sauce from a mix and topped with tiny shrimp that's been frozen for four months may sound like Heaven to the diners at Crapplebee's, but frankly, I'd trade it in a second to read that my dog is smarter than boy dogs, has minions doing her bidding, and is the fairest of them all in the kingdom of day care.

But that's just me.

If report cards weren't enough, there were party invitations, and Maeby's first one came when Lola Chanel, a Boston terrier/French bulldog mix, was turning one.

As we stood in the foyer with a dog's birthday present wrapped and bagged in my hand, dogs and people filed in and got ready for the festivities. When Mandie spotted us, I had to be quick on my feet, and this time "I forgot the money" wasn't going to fill the bill.

"I didn't know we were supposed to stay," I whispered into

Mandie's ear. "And we have a standing appointment for marriage counseling. We're learning Morse code."

"Oh, go, then, go," Mandie said kindly. "Mae will be fine. She is the teacher's pet! I'll see you back here in . . ."

"An hour?" I said, hoping I hadn't gone too far. I was also hoping that it would match the time for us to go next door, eat some lunch, and be done.

"An hour is great!" she replied, then took Maeby off to play with the other party dogs.

Apparently, however, Lola Chanel needed more than sixty minutes to get her party hoppin', the presents opened, and the kiddies on their way, because when we arrived to pick Mae up, they weren't even done with the game portion of the show yet.

"Come in, come in," Mandie said when she spied us at the door and waved us in. "You got here just in time! It's the best part!"

I can assure you that you've never lived until you have stood in a circle with ten other childless adults in their thirties and forties, clapping hands and singing "Happy Birthday" to Lola Chanel, who sits in the center, basking in all of the glory with a sensational pink feather boa twirled around her neck.

And P.S., should you, at any point, find yourself clapping hands and warbling a birthday tune to an indulged, comely only dog, don't get your hopes up. The cake on the table isn't for you.

Still, I giggled a little as Maeby ate her piece, a swash of yellow frosting smeared on her nose.

Oh boy, I thought to myself. This is fantastic! I can't wait to call Grandma when we get home.

The Bad Ass Badlands
Showdown

After living in Phoenix for more than thirty years, I wanted some rain.

I figured I was owed some rain.

So when my husband was accepted into the graduate program at an Oregon university, I almost ran there. I fantasized about summers, beautiful, magical summers in which I could actually go outside for thirty seconds without tasting my own sweat, looking at a freckle on my exposed arm, and wondering aloud, "Hmmm, does that look more like a basal or squamous cell carcinoma?" or having an earring brand and subsequently scar my neck should a gentle, though unlikely, desert breeze suddenly kick up. Summers like the ones you see on television, in which little children can play soccer in daylight without losing consciousness, or elderly people with Alzheimer's wander off into the desert on a weekly basis, never to be seen again.

On our first scouting mission, our flight was about to land at the Eugene airport when I saw that my vision was true. Green, green, green. As we drove through the small town, I saw vibrant lawn after lush lawn after emerald lawn, and I mistook it for pride of ownership until my husband reminded me that water in Oregon was something you couldn't opt out of; here it came from the sky and not a hose. Outside the room at the inn, a tree with a ten-foot circumference shaded nearly the entire building, and I was so mesmerized I called people in Phoenix and told them of the miracle I had seen. Shade. I love shade. And the shade in Eugene had no end.

"Look over there," I said to my husband as we checked out the downtown area and I pointed to a parking lot that was almost overrun by Douglas fir, oak, and maple trees. "Those are spots worth shooting over in Phoenix!" To someone who didn't know how to open an umbrella until she was thirty-three (and I only learned because I was caught in a nor'easter in New York City), I became obsessed with a new, loving climate, rushed home, and started buying rain gear. After all, a hobby is only as good as its accessories, and the same can be said for locales. With rain boots, waterproof jacket, gloves, and a Liza Minnelli assemblage of hats, I moved to Oregon.

And when I got here, I noticed that people looked at me funny, particularly the guy who installed my air conditioner in our new house (upon rolling out of Phoenix, I vowed never to be hot again, and I meant it), the hippie who fixed the sprinkler system, the man who refinished the wood floors, and the girl who colors my hair.

"Really?" they said, looking at me with skepticism, as if I was trying to pass myself off as a Hilton sister. "You moved here from Arizona? Why would you move here from Arizona? Everyone is moving from here *to* Arizona."

Every single one of them had a brother, sister, father, or close friend simply pack up and head to the land from which I just ran away. I returned their look of skepticism.

"Why? Because it's *hot* in Arizona," I'd reply. "And I am ready for a cool summer!"

"Well, in Arizona, it's a dry heat," they'd explain to me. "And it rains a lot here."

"It's not a dry heat when your thighs produce more liquid than a cow or a Slurpee machine, and that's just when you're sitting down," I'd retort. "I love it here. No one perspires and it's all green."

"But in Arizona, you can golf almost every day because the sun is shining," they'd respond. "And it's green here because it's always raining."

"Sure, you can golf every day if you drag a saline drip behind you and have your golf cart air-conditioned like the pope," I scoffed. "But it's so beautiful and shady here. Everything grows!"

"You can't golf in mud," they'd protest. "Everything turns to goop after the second day of rain, and then it goes on for six more months! It never ends!"

"Let me tell you about never ending," I cautioned. "114, 115, 116, 118, then it's 122 degrees, and that lasts for half the year! Has the Eugene airport ever shut down because the runway *melted*?"

"Wanna be on a plane that's landing on a runway covered in a sheet of ice?" they'd counter. "You don't know what the rain can do! People have to have special lamps to keep them from spiraling into a bottomless pit of depression and despair!"

"People have run out of burning houses unharmed only to get third-degree burns on their feet once they hit the sidewalks because they were barefoot," I'd volley.

"Houses sink here," they'd tell me firmly and quietly.

"People . . . *combust* there," I'd whisper.

"Yeah?" they'd conclude. "Just don't go outside without a jacket, or they might find you in five thousand years, frozen in a block of ice."

"Yeah? Well, you tell your friends that if they walk to their car from their house, bring two bottles of Aquafina!" I'd yell. "'Cause they'll need 'em!"

And then I'd add, "I found kitty mummies under my house!"

So, in the Badlands Showdown that I inevitably had time after time with my new fellow townspeople, I was never sure who won, or, for that matter, who lost: Arizona with its life-sucking heat or Oregon with its soul-drowning rain.

I do know, now that I've resided in Oregon for a while, that yeah, it takes my towels three days to dry and four months out of the year there's running water in my basement that isn't coming out of a faucet, and I was a much more successful gardener in Phoenix than I am in Eugene because I simply can't let go of the idea that plants need to be watered every day during our short summer, sometimes twice, and not once a week as my neighbors insist. And in the winter, everything, and I mean everything, squishes.

I also know that Arizona's Mexican food can't be beat, that the thirty-year expiration date on Arizona driver's licenses should be adopted as a national policy, and that sometimes, yeah, a little sun on my face feels really good.

But right now, spring just kicked the ass of winter in my wet little town and the canopy of leaves forming over my street is almost complete, leaving a cool, shady roof of green, green, and green. My neighbor Gail's peonies will be opening in a couple of weeks, and they are as big as my head. And as I look out over Eugene from my backyard deck, I can see all the way to the university, curled up at the base of a respectable-sized mountain slathered with tall Douglas firs, redwoods, and cedars, some of their trunks ten feet wide. During the rainy season, the fog curls and creeps over that mountain, and most of the time when I walk out there and see the deep-green spikes poking up out of the mist, I need to catch my breath.

It may sprinkle almost every day from November to May, but to me, it's a dry rain.

In the Basement

Before I could even get my key in the lock, the front door flew wide open and there he stood, with that look on his face.

It wasn't a good look, as I've seen that look before. It's the look that has said on various occasions, "You were right, my insurance isn't going to cover the forty-mile ambulance ride from Saguaro Lake to the hospital," "I think I just ate the last of what you wanted for lunch," "We got another letter from the IRS," or "Put a bra on. My mom is here."

"Oh boy," I said anxiously as I stepped inside, trying to figure out the disaster level of the impending scenario. "This doesn't look good. Did you read another chapter out of your Dalai Lama book, then offer a hot meal to the homeless man who does push-ups on the street without a shirt on, and he's now holed up in our bathroom because he thinks it's his cave and refuses to leave?"

"No, not after last time," he replied.

"Okay. Did you send out an e-mail to several close friends inviting them to a potluck this weekend at our house, but ended up sending it to your entire Listserv and also mistakenly forgot to include the word 'potluck'?"

"I told you, I'm very careful with the 'cc:' option in e-mail now," he insisted.

"That's good, because if any of your little college friends show up in halter tops and ask me if I'm the mom again, you're going into Laurie-imposed exile like Emily Dickinson," I added. "Well, then, I give up, unless you're tattling on Maeby because she's in your favorite reading spot and won't get up, move, or respond to you."

"She's been there *all day*," my husband informed me. "And she *won't* get up. I even tried to lure her with the leftover Chinese food, and nothing. She wouldn't even look at it!"

"Good, because I was going to have that for lunch," I said.

My husband looked away and shuffled his weight from one foot to the other.

"You didn't," I said, giving him my best "I am hungry and now I am *mad*, too," look.

"There's a problem in the basement," the love of my life said.

"If there's a shirtless man who looks like Dirty Jesus doing push-ups in my basement," I warned, "you are going out and buying new Chinese food!"

Let me say right now that I am a little timid of basements. I am not used to basements. In Phoenix, there is no soil, just the bare exposure of the earth's rocky crust, and unless you want to explode your way to middle earth and the creatures who live there, a shovel isn't going to do it. Almost no one has a basement in Phoenix except my sister-in-law, who bought her house from Mormons who procreated abundantly and needed to put seven bedrooms and a canning room bigger than half my house *somewhere*. While I embrace the idea of having another whole level of house, albeit subterranean, to store my stuff in, I know now there are dangers. If you leave stuff down there for longer than a day, you face a great risk of it getting erased from your memory altogether, and should you recall a faint memory of an object, whatever it is will emerge slightly limp, smell like my Aunt Bert's house, and have become a host to whatever it is that is growing on it.

Needless to say, I don't spend too much time down there, although that is where we keep our bikes, which is the mode of transportation my husband takes to school. He had arrived home earlier in the day and was putting his bike away when he spotted something that looked wrong.

"There was water all over the floor," he explained as we opened the door to the basement and started down the creaky wooden stairs. "It was all pooled around the drain."

And sure enough, there was a body of water in my basement, shimmering around a round hole in the floor with the top of the drain sitting off to the side of it.

"All right, stay calm, but I think something has pushed its way up from our pipes and is now hiding in the basement, and this is Oregon, land of the wet and dark, so it could be anything," I said cautiously.

"No, *I* did that," my husband replied, explaining that when he saw the puddle on the floor, he lifted up the top to the drain with his finger in order to investigate.

Then, he told me, he did what any man monkey would do and began poking around with said finger, trying to find the problem. Suddenly, he found mud.

Mud?

Hmmm, he thought to himself as he then poked around with a broom handle he found. How did *mud* get down here? And why is it shaped like that? There is mud in our basement drain? What are those white, tiny little snowflakes all around it? I must get them out, these croquette-shaped mud cakes, and I must do it with my hands. I must not wait for a second opinion. These mud balls look urgent. Because if I move them, that will clearly enable me to poke around *some more.*

So, honestly, I guess I will never know whose poo it was that he picked up, laid gently in the utility sink, and then noticed that it smelled like feces, but I hoped it was one of ours. Of course, my first question was "Well, did it look like a soft banana?" because then I could have ID'd it, but he said he wasn't really sure.

Naturally, after he realized he had fondled excrement, he scrubbed his hands until they were raw, then went to the computer to Google "Shit Diseases," which he was sure he was on the verge of getting.

"See?" he said as he held up his hands, the skin on which was merely one good rub away from sloughing off his skeletal frame.

I called my plumber, John, right away, but since it was almost sundown, he said he couldn't make it out until the next morning. In the meantime, he told me, I shouldn't flush anything unless I wanted a bigger mess, and I should be careful about even running the kitchen faucet.

My husband suggested we go out for Mexican food, and I thought that was a good idea, but as we got closer to the restaurant, I suddenly became alarmed.

"Listen," I told him. "No messing around with those tortilla chips. I don't want you handling all of them. Whatever you touch, you take. I'm not eating feces chips." And then, in a retaliatory maneuver fueled by hatred, loathing, and a decade's worth of resentment, he took his poop-fondling hand and wiped it all over my face. Since I was steering the car, there was little I could do; biting was out of the question, that would simply play into his evil hepatitis plan, so I could either careen into a KFC full of chunky middle-Americans almost exclusively dressed in tank tops or let my husband assault my head with his formerly soiled digits.

"There," he said when he was done. "Now we're both contaminated and I can touch any chip I want. And I will."

"You are a dirty man," I hissed as I parked the car in front of the restaurant.

"And you are a dirty lady," he reminded me.

"You know, I just don't understand how you ended up not only touching poop but holding on to it for so long," I finally admitted. "Why do men need to touch everything? Why can't you just look and keep your hands in your pockets? That's what they're there for, you know, so men don't go around fiddling in toilets and stroking dead things. What about a little round poop ball compelled you to reach out and feel it?"

"Oh, come on," my husband argued back, as if what I was asking was completely outrageous. "Who expects to see poop in a *basement*? Who expects to take the drain off a pipe and just have pieces of poop hanging out? I never expected that!"

"Do you really go to school?" I asked. "Or do you just huff spray paint and glue behind the 7-Eleven all day? The drain led to a sewer pipe. What did you think it led to, the Evian spring? It's the potty pipe!"

"Whatever," he said, getting out of the car. "You'll never understand. I thought it was mud. I thought they were mud patties. It was an easy mistake!"

"HA!" I bellowed, still mad about my cootie face. "I'm sorry, but I think it's safe to say I know doody when I see it!"

"So you'd think!" my husband rebutted as he opened the door to the restaurant.

• • •

The next day, I was barely out of bed when John was at the front door, ready to investigate. I showed him the pond in the basement and told him to be careful.

"It's a shit hole," I explained, hoping to get a laugh.

"What?" John said, squinting, not even remotely entertaining me.

"There's poop down there," I explained. "I know because my husband touched it."

"Why'd he do that?" he replied, visibly recoiling.

I shrugged. "He thought it was mud," I said kindly.

"That's not mud!" he replied. "What would make mud look like that, in a little patty?"

"Believe me, I'm thinking the same thing," I agreed. "But if you find any red mice in the drain, *they are not mine.* I know better!"

John responded by giving me a look that said, "*I am not coming here anymore.*"

Upon examination and with the use of a heavy-duty plumber's snake, he determined that the clog was not a gigantic poop ball, or a colony of mysterious red mice, but roots. Nothing but tree roots that the snake had now thrashed away, leaving a clear, unobstructed path from my toilet to the great unknown.

"Here. These are for your husband," John said as he handed

me a pair of floppy, white latex gloves on his way out. "In case he feels the urge again."

All of the hubbub about the basement made me a little more aware that it was something I needed to pay attention to, so several weeks later when I heard some loud splashing coming from that direction as I was doing the laundry, I ran down there immediately. Sure enough, while a lake hadn't formed on the floor of the basement, one was getting ready to as the utility sink was about to spill over with water drained from the washer. I almost reached for a bottle of Drano on the shelf when I spied the broom handle and sort of poked around the drain of the sink. Quickly, I heard the water begin to rush through the pipes. I sighed a breath of relief, stood back, and watched the water flush down.

That's so weird, I thought to myself. What could have been covering the drain—a piece of paper, maybe some cardboard or packing materials that had fallen into the sink? I wouldn't doubt it at all with all of the stuff we have down here. I watched as the last of the water trickled down, crisis averted, and there I saw a form emerge, almost like a golf ball. A golf ball? I thought to myself. Could it be one of Maeby's balls, totally encrusted with dirt? Why would one of Maeby's balls be in the utility sink? Plus, I don't remember her having toys that small, she should never have toys that small, Oprah's dog choked on a ball that small and died, I kept thinking as my hands moved toward it to pick it up, closer, closer, closer, and then I saw a second golf ball, closer, closer, it almost looks like a chocolate truffle, or a croque—

"Oh, shit!" I screamed shrilly as I yanked my own hand away, just in the nick of time.

And, on second glance, I saw that I was absolutely right.

Blue-Light Special

I love a good sale, just like anybody, but there are just some things I can't bring myself to skimp on.

In Phuket (I don't know how you pronounce it correctly, but I've been doing it phonetically for the last hour and am getting a big kick out of it), an internationally popular resort island in southern Thailand, blue Hawaiians on the beach aren't the only things you can get for cheap. Apparently, Phuket (isn't that fun?) has seen a boom in the number of private clinics specializing in cosmetic surgery and sex-change operations for tourists because the costs for those procedures are far lower than in the United States or Europe.

Now, honestly, the last thing I'd bargain-hunt for would be a new nose, brighter eyes, or a whole set of genitals. Those are examples of things I wouldn't use a coupon for. Sure, if they have a two-for-one dinner at a Sizzler on Phuket, count me in, but clearly, I wouldn't use the same discount should Laurie want to become Larry, if you know what I mean. They don't call that stuff the family jewels for nothing. Ever hear of the expression "You get what you pay for"? Well, it's true. Do you want to spend the rest of your life explaining, "Yeah, well, they're not exactly what you would call a matching pair, but the one that causes that exact reaction was 20 percent off!"

I mean, sure, when you're in the market for a book, a sweater, or even a bra, seconds will do, but when you're playing outlet mall with your gender, *who knows* what you'll wake up as? You might become a whole new species, something even *Star Trek: The Next Generation* hasn't seen. Someone I used to work with in Phoenix decided Tijuana was the place that they were going to go to obtain lap-band surgery because it was considerably cheaper there. The details were then revealed: the procedure wasn't even going to take place in a hospital but would be done in a hotel, and even though I think Holiday Inn Express commercials are funny, I understand that they are just commercials and that Holiday Inn isn't a college or a medical school, even in Spanish. Weeks after the surgery when the person was eating at a restaurant, the patient followed the doctor's orders and ordered the soup—then proceeded to gobble up artichoke dip, eight squares of pita bread, and seven deep-fried coconut shrimp. You get what you pay for, I thought to myself; Dr. Holiday Inn Express slipped you a roofie, knicked your belly button with an X-Acto blade, gave you a Band-Aid, and then cashed your check. You don't even have as much as a twist tie in there, let alone a lap band.

When thinking about doing something permanent, irreversible, and requiring more talent and skill than coloring hair, I tend to take the approach that you're gonna need the best guy possible. If I'm considering a body-altering procedure, I'll save my pennies, eat out one or two fewer meals a week, stop shopping at Gap and go to Target instead because I want Dr. Number One.

I don't want Dr. Half Price, I want the best guy on the block. He may be *from* Thailand, but if he's that good, he's not there anymore.

And if that's not bad enough, it's in *Thailand*. No way am I going there, no matter how big my chin collection has grown. I saw *Brokedown Palace* sixteen times last month on HBO, and if that country will arrest Claire Danes, it will arrest anybody. No one is safe, and I'll be damned if I spend one night of my life sleeping outside on a straw mat with roaches trying to crawl into my ears and parasites attempting to stage a military coup in my small intestine.

Should I decide that I need some work done someday, I'll find a nice doctor in a white coat who has an office with walls. And if my insurance won't cover the surgery and I can't afford it, I'm not going to Thailand. I guess I'd rather just say, "All right, then. Phuket."

The Idiot Girl and
the Flaming Tantrum
of Death

I **will be** the first one to admit that I was one to think that I had done a pretty good job of hanging on to my "cool" quotient after I finished college, got married, found a job, bought a house, and then started wearing body shapers. I will fully cop to having the idea that should I ever return to a college campus, I could slip right in, fit in amongst the younguns without any problem or hiccup because I thought I knew what was goin' on.

In fact, every now and then, I still go to see bands if one of my favorites is playing (although now I like to leave a little bit before the show is over to beat the traffic out of the parking lot), I can still slug down JD with the best of them (although now I really prefer a nice red wine coupled with an Ambien), and I prefer the Gap to Chico's any day (although I do adore the room that anything marked "stretch" affords me).

So if you hold that delightful, youthful reverie close to your self-esteem, identity, and/or worth as a human being and believe it as much as I did, then my advice to you is that unless you really want to know just how old you are, a college campus is the last place you'd ever want to be. Retain your dream, full and intact, and go to a golf course instead, mutter "Fascists" under your breath as you're teeing off, or eat lunch at a Cheesecake Factory and pretend to be horrified that people are delighted to pay seven dollars for a piece of cake.

However, no one had given me that advice before I moved to a college town that every September doubles its population from the preceding month's. Therefore, I was entirely unprepared for what I saw the first time I went to pick my husband up at the university.

Those children were naked.

"Those children are naked!" I exclaimed, my jaw dropped, as he got into the car.

"Oh, it was cold this morning," he said as he shook his head. "You should have seen what happens on a hot day. It looks like lunchtime at a Roman bathhouse."

"Why doesn't someone *do* something?" I cried.

"Like what?" my husband said, laughing.

"I don't know," I said, shaking my head, then spotted a girl who was wearing a red bandana as a shirt. "Institute a 'clothing mandatory' rule? Napkins are not apparel! That's not from the Gap! You can't get that at the Gap! I was just there!"

"Why are you freaking out?" my husband asked.

"Because it's a college campus, not a strip club named Jiggles!" I exclaimed. "I would never wear that! She could at least have two bandanas, one for each chichi! That girl has banana boobs, too. A bra would be to her benefit."

"Oh," my husband said with a pass of his hand. "The returning adult students don't dress like that. They dress like you."

And just like that, with a long squeak and several pops, I felt the air dribble out of my coolness balloon like a slow, old, strangled fart, stopping every now and then to catch its breath until, with one last rumble, it emptied with an exhausted *fffffuuuuuuuu-uuhhhhh*.

It served me right, I knew. I thought I could be college-aged cool? I thought I still had that? I can't even eat caramel anymore because the chances are good to great that it will pull out my remaining teeth, most of which are composed of some sort of composite material that's a close cousin to Rubbermaid products.

After all, I should have realized I had not only conquered the pinnacle of adulthood but had firmly cemented myself in middle age when Atlas Van Lines showed up to move my stuff. The last time I'd changed residential locations, I'd rented a U-Haul, which in my opinion was still very much under the governing guidelines of youth and young adulthood, and even that, I thought, was a huge leap considering that when I moved out of my parents' house, I simply threw a heap of black clothes into the backseat and drove off.

"When was the last time you were on a college campus?" my husband asked me, shocked that I was so shocked.

"I don't know," I replied, trying to think. "Probably . . ."

He shook his head. "When you were in college?" he asked. "Boys still had posters of Tawny Kitaen up in their dorm rooms when you were in college. Boys still *looked* like Tawny Kitaen when you were in college. Things have changed," he advised me. "You have dental insurance now, and you drive a Prius."

"So?" I shot back defensively. "What does that mean?"

"Can't be bad ass in a Prius" was all he said.

"Whatever," I replied, trying to ignore him. But I had already realized that was true on the freeway one day when a guy in a Dodge Ram truck with California plates was tailgating me so closely I could see the spittle from his chew run down his chin in my rearview mirror, and when I didn't go fast enough for him, he pulled ahead of me and then abruptly cut me off, apparently to teach me a lesson about driving in front of a man who can't even keep brown saliva contained in his mouth. It was at that moment that I understood there was absolutely nothing I could do to retaliate, there was no category of road rage that you can fit a Prius into even if you were blasting Black Sabbath on your factory-installed two-speaker stereo. No matter how you cut it, you'd still have the ferocity of Lovey Howell in a floppy straw hat holding a mai tai. I mean, what was I going to do, pull up next to him and shout, "Hey, asshole! Think you're so tough, huh? Well, I'm getting ninety-nine miles to the gallon at this very minute according to my energy-consumption monitor! Wait—now it's seventy-five. No, sixty-four. Okay, back up to ninety-two. Point is, I could drive to *Florida* on a full tank! And I don't mean Jacksonville, I mean *Miami*! Whooz the big boy now, huh, punk?"

And besides, even if you truly were a Bad Ass in Eugene, I seriously don't even know where you'd go to put your Bad Assness on display to create the appropriate response of awe and fear in order to meet Bad Ass guidelines and retain your status. It's a quiet little town full of old hippies, college professors, and solar-energy enthusiasts. Naming their children insidiously damaging names (Ptolemy, Star, Alchemy) and breast-feeding until the second grade are the typical, biggest, and brashest ways people outdo each other. I guess if you were a Bad Ass and desperately needed an outlet, there's always the Saturday Market, where you could take your frustrations and inner bastard out on an organic tomato or a loaf of gluten-free bread, but then you risk being pecked to death by the passive-aggressive comments of passersby, including the observation that a Bad Ass came to the market "and didn't even bring his own canvas bag!"

Things like invasion of personal space and talking in movie theaters were at state-of-emergency levels in my new hometown precisely because people knew that there is generally no one who will threaten harm or, even worse, confront them when they violate social boundaries. This, of course, isn't counting the meth addicts, who due to either the abundance of rain and mold or the lack of available sunshine have evolved into a subspecies that knows no rival, resilient to both discomfort and authority, kind of like an Ultimate Tweaker. Sure, tweakers wreak havoc everywhere, but in the Pacific Northwest, their powers are legendary. I saw one guy on the news in Portland who barricaded himself in his lab/apartment for several hours and didn't come out until the police had thrown in the *seventh* tear-gas bomb and even then it still took five cops to get him onto the ground and cuffed. If there was a National Tweaker Olympics, Oregon would bring home the gold in every category (Living in Squalor, Poisoning Your Neighbors, Developing Facial Scabs, Public Aggression, Theft of Useless Things, Taking Stuff Apart, and Crazy Talking).

Aside from the meth crowd, though, Eugene was a mellow, easy place, to the extent that I realized even my husband would win a bar fight here. All he'd have to do is stand up and the whole scuffle would be over. I was seriously concerned about how I would fit in until one day I found myself standing on a corner downtown, loudly booing, hissing, and giving a very enthusiastic thumbs-down to a Hummer that had happened to get stuck at a red light, and I knew then that my transformation was complete. I found Eugene to be a great change of pace from our former life in Phoenix, and in every respect it was ideal (especially publicly booing conservatives driving excessively large cars), until that day when I picked my husband up at school and saw what youth really looked like instead of the way I remembered it.

The thing was that I didn't feel any different than I did when I was twenty. I would probably no longer move into a house with seven guys that I barely knew, none of whom had any visible means of support, and a boyfriend whose biggest investments to date were a rather large snake and a gray-primered Volkswagen with only one seat. In addition and with the advantage of hindsight, grabbing a clean set of sheets from my mother's linen closet along with my collection of mourning clothes would certainly have had its benefits. Okay, okay, maybe not twenty. It's twenty-five that I didn't feel any different from, but wait, that was around the time I dated the bong boy with the "learning disability" and I was kicked out of the third community college in a row. Thirty. I don't feel any different from when I was thirty, but then again, I bought a HUD house in a bad neighborhood across the street from a lady with a shelter's worth of diseased cats.

Thirty-five.

YES. *Thirty-five.*

I don't feel any different from when I was thirty-five.

"I am still cool," I informed my husband as we drove away

from campus. "I don't feel any different from when I was thirty-five."

"Your dental records would tell a different story," he inserted.

"I can't wait to laugh at you when a pork chop rips out your first molar," I said with a smirk. "Just wait. It'll happen."

"Well, I guess you really haven't changed much since then," he agreed. "When you were thirty-five, chances were good we'd spend a Saturday night the way we spent last Saturday night, at Safeway looking for Gas-X and you complaining to the cashier that they stopped carrying the Gas-X melty strips, which was criminal because they worked 'so much faster and with unprecedented ease.'"

Because, really, who wants to be twenty again, I thought, living in a house with a bunch of dirty guys and a snake? Who wants to be thrown out of community college for the third time, working a minimum-wage job? Who wants to move into an abandoned, worn-down house in a shitty neighborhood because that's the only place you can afford to live?

Don't get me wrong. I loved the reckless abandon of my younger, skinnier, prettier, poorer days, but doing all of that once in a lifetime was pretty much enough. I loved being thirty-five, even if it did mean getting some gray hair, growing a blap (a belly and a lap merging as one, a term coined by my friend, Sharron) and wearing a body shaper. I loved my age now. I loved where I was.

And I loved driving a Prius. People smile when they see you and almost always let you in during traffic.

I was driving that same Prius several days later when I was coming back from the market. I decided to take a back residential street rather than a major so that I could make a right-hand turn as opposed to a left. Now, this is a narrow road that cuts a straight line through the neighborhood; it is so small it doesn't even have any lines painted down the middle, and most of it is downhill. It has speed bumps, and several hand-painted signs reminding people to slow down and that children are playing and being breast-fed.

Personally, I didn't see a need to speed down this street, but even though I didn't have my foot on the gas, traveling downhill I was going about thirty miles per hour, which is about as fast as you can go anywhere in Eugene unless you're on the freeway. So I braked a couple of times, because Priuses are rather quiet cars and are no friend to the blind, people using iPods, people on cell phones, and, sadly, squirrels.

My concern for not only playing neighborhood children but the now teetering-on-the-brink-of-extinction Eugene squirrel, however, was not good news to the shiny, black Volkswagen Jetta behind me, which, to be frank, was acting a little like a bull, I'm a cow, and there's been an inappropriate amount of drinking going on.

I descended the hill and approached the street where I needed to make a right, put on my blinker, slowed down, and started to make the turn when the Jetta passed me, honking loudly, and the passenger—a college-aged hippie with ratted, matted hair, screamed out the passenger window, "What the fu——?" and threw her hands up.

At me. So, instincts being what they are, I flipped her off without consideration because it's the sharpest reflex I have, and before it even hit me what had just happened.

She was young, I was not, and I was driving a Prius. To her, insulting me was the safest thing in the world.

Much to her chagrin, however, the old lady in the spineless car really still was the twenty-year-old who threw her black Sisters of Mercy clothes into the back of a car and left her parents' house to live with dirty boys in a punk band and a snake. And the old, slowpoke shriv who was hitting her brakes every ten seconds to keep the children and squirrels safe was the same girl who lived for nearly a decade in a craptastic neighborhood where she heard gunshots with more frequency than she heard birds, chased packs of wild dogs off her porch, hired local drug addicts as handymen, and was entirely unafraid of two privileged brats in a brand-new German car. Because now, you see, the brazen yet ridiculously stupid hippie chick in a black shiny Jetta had just foolishly activated the Flaming Tantrum of Death because Lady Prius was also the same old bat whose gastrointestinal workings still felt like she ate a broccoli farm because Safeway was out of melty strips on Saturday and as a result, she thoroughly believed that the possibility that she would project fire out of her ass was not at all unlikely because she was bloated, gassy, and now her pilot light had been lit.

Backstory: The Flaming Tantrum of Death was born one afternoon after witnessing one of the most spectacular flameouts/hissy fits in world history. After a former acquaintance of mine decided that writing impolite bulletins about other people and posting them on the Internet would be a productive use of spare time, there was no response from anyone who had been targeted in the tirades. So the author then e-mailed the bulletins to those being insulted, including me, to ensure that they were seen, which prompted my astute and observant friend Lore to comment sarcastically, "Just in case you didn't notice my Flaming Tantrum of Death, here it is!" Now, it's never nice to make fun of someone having a full-blown, Target toy-aisle "Mommy Buy This for Me!" meltdown, but the truth of the matter is that when the person in question has put a bull's-eye on you, you can either become offended or see it as the high-caliber, Las Vegas–style entertainment that it is.

So despite the fact that the entire episode was both embarrassing and tedious to witness, it was spellbinding and spectacular in its absurdity, which is to say you could likely throw the equivalent of seven tear-gas bombs at it and it would still crawl back to e-mail you another spiteful comment. The Flaming Tantrum of Death raised anger and revenge to a new plateau, and with proper usage, it is something to aspire to, mixing seventh-grade rage with the resilience of Tempur-Pedic technology. In awe of its inspiring power, my friends and I decided to take possession of it and harness it, deliver it from evil and use it only for good, as in terrorizing two damn dirty hippies who deserved to be touched by its terrifying potency.

If you're wondering what a Flaming Tantrum of Death looks like in its physical form, it very much resembles me abandoning that right-hand turn and furiously flipping my car around to follow a shiny black Jetta and the hippies inside it, who, it was apparent, were laughing, laughing, laughing at Lady Prius until they saw her directly behind them in their rearview mirror and became suddenly still because unfortunately for them, they were stuck at a red light and never once thought that Lady Prius had the ability to terrorize anyone, let alone have the temperament and mean streak of Sonny Corleone, except that I was wearing something more than an undershirt, which, I admit, lessened the Tantrum's impact substantially.

And because the hippies were so fond of honking, the Flaming Tantrum of Death progressed to its second stage as I laid on my horn, my palm pressed firmly and absolutely into the center of my steering wheel, where I let it trumpet continuously without letting up while I cackled, "Don't you love it? Don't you love honking? You're so good at it, you little honkers! Do you like people honking at you? Do you? How 'bout I honk this horn until I get out of this fussy Prius, come over there and rip the filthy hippie dreadlocks off your head, go home and sand down a dresser with them?" (We all know that I probably wasn't going to do that because as soon as I got over there, the light would turn green and I'd be standing in an intersection like a lunatic fighting myself, but it sounded so good and quite dramatic, so I had to say it.)

And initially, both the girl and the boy hippie simply sat there dumbfounded as the horn blared until they decided upon their method of retaliation and began moving their arms and torsos from side to side and all around in the weapon of mass destruction known as "interpretive dance."

They were both *dancing*, like "Grateful Dead, I just ate a loaded brownie, let's go feed the homeless and then sit naked in an endangered tree" dancing.

"Is that all you've got?" I yelled. "You're going to DANCE at me? Big horn honkers, 'What the fu—?' screamers, brazen tailgaters can only DANCE at me? Well, dance to this, you smelly tofu assholes! You're wearing a bandana shirt, aren't you? Dance, hippies, dance!"

And I laid on the horn again and didn't let up. And I kept it going until the light turned green, they made a right, I made a right, and then they ran the next red trying to get away from me.

I guess they were tired of dancing.

Now, I was fully aware that in the next day's Eugene newspaper, the front-page headline was most likely to read PRIUS OWNER NEEDS ANGER MANAGEMENT THERAPY AND A HUG, PERHAPS LESS SODIUM, but I could not care less. Maybe it was just about time that a Prius owner went batshit, just to show that it could be done. And so that peace-loving, tree-sitting, college-aged damn dirty hippies would think twice before yelling, "What the fu——?" to a woman in a hybrid, driving the speed limit and trying not to squash a kid or small woodland creature, even if she was getting ninety-nine miles to the gallon while doing it.

And, just for the record, I am still looking for that car. It's a small enough town. I'll find it.

I happen to have some fire tantrum left in me to breathe— just enough to make some hippies dance.

Come Sail Away

For a fraction of a second, as the raft teetered over the edge of the thrashing, churning, foaming waters below, I knew that I had made an enormous mistake.

I didn't have time to do anything—not to look at Jamie, who I hoped was still sitting to my right, not to yell "I hate *all* of you!" to the rest of the people crammed behind us in the raft, not even to take a breath—before we dove in furiously, meeting a wall of silty, pearly, thirty-three-degree water that rolled over us without a slice of hesitation or mercy.

Somehow I know that when we were sitting in front of Jamie's computer in her new house in Portland a month prior, neither one of us pictured that in a matter of weeks, we would be clinging to a piece of plywood with frozen fingers, trying not to get thrown overboard to meet our destiny on the tip of a sharp rock. I know for a fact that scenario never crossed our minds as we chose the activities we would pursue during our much anticipated cruise to Alaska.

"For our port of call in Juneau, this excursion has 'crackers, a gourmet selection of cheeses, artisan sausages, and hot apple cider in the bunkhouse as we conclude our relaxing, hypnotic river journey,'" I remember her reading off the computer screen. "Which do you think sounds better, that one, or the one where we 'experience the landscape and vistas during a ten-mile bike ride, with a warming treat of fresh-baked chocolate chip cookies and hot cocoa at the base of the glacier'?"

"Don't get me wrong," I offered. "I love a solid chocolate chip cookie, but if I'm riding ten miles for a treat, at the end of that road better be the Keebler Forest, where I have an open invitation to gorge on a vast variety of baked goods until my guts explode. And I get to keep an elf."

"Have you noticed the square footage of our cabin?" Jamie reminded me. "There's no room for another body, even a rosy, fleshy master crafter of chocolate-covered graham crackers. I don't care if such artisan is the size of a two-year-old."

"It *is* small," I agreed. "I've worn underwear that could fit more people in it. But my sincere hope is that we have so much fun repeatedly pillaging the buffet that we won't even notice that we're sharing quarters the size of the brig on the space shuttle."

And honestly, almost the minute we set foot on that ship, I knew I was right. As soon as we were on the gangway, the element of fun collapsed and rolled over at our feet, eager to please us and fulfill any command that popped into our heads. As we sat at our table in the nearly empty buffet dining room, we marveled over the pristine selection of delicious treats presented for our enjoyment. We were so excited to begin our vacation, we got there early enough to be one of the first people on board and thus among the first beholders of the buffet, which was magnificent and royal in itself. In the dining room we sampled pickings from our plates of bounty—each tastefully heaped with the appropriate amount of salad, delicious salted meats, imported cheeses, and the finest in accoutrements—including fruit, macaroni and cheese, a pancake, some roast beef, a bowl of French onion soup, three kinds of pickles, a cracker assortment, a quail's egg, a barbeque rib, a chocolate mousse cup, a tandoori chicken leg and an ice cream sundae—as we looked out over the Puget Sound from the dining room window, full of calm, serenity, and wonder.

"At home, we live like peasants," I announced disgustedly, referring not only to the food bonanza but also to the way that every crew member smiled at us, held doors open, provided us with hand sanitizer, and cheerfully and earnestly asked us how we were every time we saw them. I ripped into the orange flesh of the chicken leg and shoved another pickle into my mouth. "We were made for this kind of life. I already know I never want to get off this ship. Kicking and screaming is the way I bet it will go down. Maybe I'll just get a job here. I can be the free-ice-cream girl, or the pickle organizer."

"Mmmmm," Jamie hummed as she shook her head after a delicate bite of her tiny ham sandwich on a petite baguette. "I'd think about that if I were you. I saw a documentary on the Travel Channel about the real life of cruise ships, and from that angle, it doesn't look too inviting. The employees live below sea level where there aren't any windows, and they sleep in shifts because they are forced to share beds."

"We had to sleep in bunk beds at Girl Scout camp," I offered.

"Not quite the same thing as lying in the sweat of Lars, the potato and carrot peeler, and trying to go to sleep on a pillow that's already been drooled on for eight hours by someone with questionable dental hygiene," my best friend replied.

"So you'd think," I volleyed as I chomped on the rib. "But Shari Greene took the top bunk above me and then had a nocturnal accident typically reserved for toddlers, the elderly, and middle-aged homeless men passed out on flattened cardboard boxes behind Popeyes Chicken. There is no badge for that, you know. I had no idea what to do, I was not prepared! I spent the rest of the night huddled in the corner with my mouth closed very tightly. I was almost positive the sun was never going to come up."

"Wasn't she the one who told Mrs. Henry's fourth-grade class that Christmas was a lie because there was no Santa Claus, something that the more sensitive and reality-delayed, especially concerning the existence of fantasy creatures and humanoid characters with magic abilities, students weren't quite ready to hear?" Jamie asked.

"Didn't want to talk about it then," I reminded her as I killed the mousse cup in one big lick. "Don't want to talk about it now."

"And wasn't she the one who was on the same relay team you were an alternate for in our fifth-grade class?" Jamie asked, and she nibbled on a piece of lettuce. "And got so sick right before the race that you got her spot and then won the race for the team?"

"That will teach her to eat a second bean burrito, a taco, and the fiesta pineapple upside-down cake from my lunch after she already scarfed down her own school lunch," I commented as I grinned. "Oink, oink, little pig! The only thing I regret is that I didn't make her eat it under a drunk hobo sleeping on a grate."

"I thought your only regret was lying to God after you knelt down before the race began and promised the Lord that you'd become a nun if you won first place," Jamie recalled. "Sister Laurie Ann."

"Intentionally overfeeding the third leg runner with a free second lunch that would obviously lead to extreme gastrointestinal distress was clearly the devil's work," I assured her as I finished off my ice cream sundae. "Who wants a nun who at ten was seeking revenge with a weapon of a fiesta pineapple upside-down cake? I bet even Jeffrey Dahmer was nicer on Field Day than I was."

Just then, we heard a series of three soft chimes from the overhead speaker, accompanied by the voice of Devon, the portly and perky British cruise director who had greeted us when we boarded the ship, letting us know that all of our cabins were ready for occupancy.

Both Jamie and I gasped as we pushed away our lunch dishes and grabbed our purses.

"All I know is that if there are bunk beds in there," she informed me, "I'm getting the top one after what you just ate. I'm not spending the night huddled in the corner after acid reflux and the sea tag-team you."

As soon as we opened the door to our cabin, we both saw that Jamie was right: I couldn't have kept the elf, not even if he fit in a drawer. In fact, our cabin space was so economical that one of us had to step aside if the other one wanted to go anywhere, even to bed. It was so incredibly tiny that no matter where you were in the room, you were touching something. Whether it was my arm, my skull, or the front-runner, my butt, some part of me was constantly touching *something*.

"Thank God I left my cords at home, " I mentioned. "The drywall would have been sanded down to studs within hours."

"What's the deal with the bed?" Jamie asked, nodding her head over to the queen-sized mattress and not the two twins we had requested. "You gotta be kidding me. It's bad enough that you made me buy all of the exact clothes for this cruise that you bought, but I did not sign up for a 'together' vacation. The two ladies next door look like Drew Carey and Ron Reagan, so if there is something you need to tell me, say it now while I can still jump overboard."

"But I'm a good spooner," I joked. "Ask anyone I've been on vacation with! I promise I reserved a cabin with twin beds. I'll see if this bed comes apart and you look behind those curtains. Maybe there's a small sleeping area behind them."

Jamie swung the draperies open, flooding sunlight into the room as I lifted the comforter to expose two single beds pushed together to form one.

"I didn't find a bed," Jamie exclaimed. "But I did find the balcony! It's almost as big as our room!"

"Yes, and we'll still have to take turns standing out there," I commented. "Unless spooning isn't *completely* off the table."

After I called the housekeeping line and asked to have two sets of linens brought up, I fell back on the beds and touched all four walls at the same time with either a foot or a hand.

"What do you want to do for dinner tonight?" I asked Jamie. "We could revisit the glorious buffet, or we could try one of the restaurants onboard."

"Mmmm, the buffet," Jamie said as she thought from the balcony. "It was an extraordinary spread of delicacies and fried foods alike. I wouldn't mind going back there at all."

"Sounds good to me," I agreed. "How's the balcony?"

"Time to rotate," she said. "I just saw a seagull that looked awfully familiar, and it saw me."

Just as Jamie and I were engaged in an act of no-contact spooning over the threshold of the balcony as we attempted to change places, there was a knock at the door.

We both paused for several seconds and stood very still.

"Okay, listen," Jamie finally said. "There is no room in this cabin for regulated personal space, and we are currently in the most challeging Twister position known to man. There's no way to get out of this clean. Let's count to three and make a break for it, and I apologize ahead of time for whichever body part I Bad Touch you on."

"Likewise," I agreed. "Whichever base we get to, I will not read anything but necessity into it. One, two, three!"

With Jamie flying north and me jumping south, we shot apart like a pair of magnets repelling each other as Jamie bounced off the cabin door and I landed on the balcony.

Jamie opened the door and there stood two young men, one tall and one short, with the smaller one holding some nice, clean, passenger-quality white sheets and the other one carrying two plush, puffy comforters.

"Hello," the shorter one said with the nice, warm smile we had seen replicated on faces all over the ship, worn by anyone wearing a uniform of any type. "You called to get the bed separated? We are your stewards. I am Ardhi from Indonesia."

"I am James from Jamaica," the taller one followed.

Jamie turned and looked on me with a smile that said exactly what I was feeling.

Holy shit, we have servants!!!!

I have never, in all of my experiences on earth, felt more elated.

It was better than turning nine and seeing the hulking silhouette of a wrapped Barbie townhouse next to your birthday cake. It was more incredible than realizing that the guy who just asked you to marry him was no less than 68 percent sober. It was more amazing than not only eating the most delicious and high-fat-content meals of all time and steamrolling on to an equally guilt-infused dessert, but then also not having to work the calories off on the treadmill because you lost them by getting a mixed-cocktail-inspired flu.

"I feel like we're in a Merchant Ivory movie!" Jamie whispered as she sidled up against the wall to permit our butlers entrance.

"I'm Laurie," I said as I waved from the balcony. "I'd come closer but I'd be arrested for some garden-variety assault."

"Thank you for coming so quickly," Jamie added. "I'm Jamie, and you just saved our friendship."

"Yes," I agreed. "The last thing we wanted to do on this ship was share a bed!"

From the doorway of the bathroom, Jamie leaned out and gave me a stern look.

"Don't," it said. "Please don't. Let me enjoy this for at least a minute more, because I will never be here again. I will never be sitting on a bathroom sink with my feet propped up on the toilet lid watching my butlers change my sheets *again*. PLEASE."

But the duration of the silence in our cabin continued for too long as the stewards split the bed apart into two smaller ones and left a cavern of wonder and speculation wide open and ready to be spelunked into. It was like a fluffy, perfect mound of whipped cream just demanding to be demolished. And I was just the one to kick the air out of it.

"Jamie watched a behind-the-scenes show about cruise ships and their working conditions," I ventured as Jamie rolled her eyes and shook her head at me. "The show reported that cruise ship employees have to share a bed."

Ardhi and James looked at each other but didn't stop working. Ardhi smiled at me, then nodded. "Yes, we do," he confirmed.

"You're kidding," I replied. "Even on this ship? I thought it might be true of the Disney cruises, because Disney even makes their characters share underwear and the creepy crawlies, like Pooh Lice, that come with them, but I didn't think *this* cruise line would! They make their commercials seem so love-filled and friendly, like a place that would provide a bug-free bed for everybody, or at least a can of personal pesticide!"

Sensing a sympathetic ear, James piped up as he continued making up one of the separated beds. "Not only do we share a bed, but we sleep in shifts. We share with three other people, taking turns."

"What happens if the person before you is a lazy bed sharer and hasn't changed the sheets before it's your sleepy shift?" I asked. "And please tell me you don't have to share a pillow!"

Ardhi and James simply burst out laughing. Although we hadn't set sail, I was very unsure whether it was sea sickness or revulsion that had just socked me in the gut.

"Do you share a bed with the captain?" I prodded, eager to gross myself out further. "Or Devon? I'd bet he never changes the sheets and he produces a wide variety of nighttime noises."

Both Ardhi and James giggled again but said nothing.

"Where do you eat?" I pressed further. "Do you eat at the buffet?"

"No, no, no." James smiled as he shook his head and tucked the last edge of the sheet under the mattress. "We have a cafeteria on our deck. We aren't allowed up to the passenger buffet. We would lose our jobs if we did that."

"Do you have the same food there as we have?" I asked hopefully.

"No," Ardhi replied slowly, and then added a chuckle as he flung out a comforter on one of the beds. "It's not the same food. It's not very good down there. Hot dogs and things you microwave."

James nodded his head in agreement.

"You know what I think," I replied, despite the fact that I knew by the silence that was sitting on the bathroom sink that I had said enough already. "I think you should get a drool-free pillow! You deserve a clean pillow. Everyone does!"

"Your beds are ready!" Ardhi said as he straightened out the last wrinkle on a comforter. "Embarkation is always very busy for us. Have a great dinner!"

And with a little wave, Ardhi and James shuffled out of the room in short, little steps and closed the door behind them. Immediately Jamie poked her head out of the bathroom doorway.

"All of the asshole colonialists in the room raise their hands," I announced as my arm sliced into the air.

"God job, César Chávez!" Jamie said as she hopped off the sink. "Who do you think you are, every disenfranchised college-aged male trying to establish his identity by hanging a Che Guevara poster in his dorm room and keeping a beat-up copy of *On the Road* in his backpack? Do you want to see those boys left on the pier with sad Ardhi and James faces as we leave the next port?"

"No, but I feel so bad for them," I replied. "They are both so nice."

"We can do other things for them besides urging them to unionize! We can leave them a big tip at the end, and proclaim their excellent customer service on comment cards. But this ship is not an American ship, and they play by different rules. And the last time I heard, there were no unions in Jamaica or Indonesia, and sharing a pillow was probably not a big deal until you brought it up and mentioned slobber. I'm ready for the buffet, but I will only eat dinner with you if there's a promise of not mentioning boycotting grapes to anyone working near or around the salad menagerie and fruit carousel. No hissy fits, provoked or otherwise. Agreed?"

Stymied, I nodded my head, but the moment after we entered the buffet dining room, I knew all bets were off. What I witnessed there was unbelievable. I have honestly only seen that kind of chaos on news footage when the United Nations drops sacks of rice and grain into the middle of a country experiencing prolonged famine or when the Marines pull out of a war zone and there's one helicopter for the 10,000 civilians attempting to escape with them. Typically, Americans are only most likely to behave in a manner that frantic if they are exposed to something free and sample-sized, but clearly, in the gauntlet that formerly was a buffet line, the passengers lost sight of the fact that they had already paid for the food they were swarming on, which under normal circumstances usually takes the thrill right out of the hunt. Willful ignorance prevailed as the buffet that we had visited earlier in the day became not even remotely recognizable; people elbowed each other in an attempt to outnudge everyone else to the vat of macaroni salad; dirty looks were exchanged when a desired piece of fried chicken was plucked from the poultry mountain by a fellow marauder; and faces were concealed behind towers of brisket and barbecued ribs piled onto dishes as passengers uneasily wavered in a balancing act to an empty spot at a table.

I have to be honest and say that all of the food that was wonderfully desirable only hours earlier lost all its appeal once it was apparent I would have to fight for my meal. I felt like a Christian in the Colosseum, on display and ready to die for my belief in a ciabatta roll. A mere three seconds after we got in line, I was separated from my friend by the hungry hordes swathed in Wal-Mart resort wear, and my pledge to her was challenged by a man who, at the salad menagerie, dug his virus- and bacteria-laden hand into the raisin bowl to scoop up a dozen or so wrinkly nuggets, only to delicately place them on the community spoon provided for his protection and *then* transfer them to his plate. When he turned around to leave and search out additional food to fondle, my eyes were still wide with horror and my jaw gaping, and when he looked at me for a brief split second, I had no control over my innate reaction to throw him an expression of disgust and cry "YUCK!" over the din of serving spoons clinking on china.

When I finally found Jamie at the fruit carousel twenty minutes later, my plate was empty and so was my reserve of fear concerning blatant confrontation. I had been pushed, cut in front of, and stared down by fellow passengers, including a streetwise sixth grader who should have been in school to begin with but apparently had the identical attraction for the same mini quiche Lorraine that I did. I was ready to bite someone. I was able to calm down a bit after I spied triangles of juicy, blood-red watermelon lined up like fallen dominoes on a silver tray. They looked so refreshing and delicious and serene, just waiting for me to reach forward and pluck one. I was going in with a pair of tongs when the woman in front emitted a throaty gargle and open-mouthed coughed, sending a direct hit in on the pineapple, the grapes, and my watermelon, all of which now fully deserved boycotting.

"Jamie," I yelled in a booming voice to my friend and everyone between us, "avoid the Tropical Delights Tray! This one in front of me just coughed all over it like she was a terrorist. I can see little noroviruses—which cause nausea, vomiting, and diarrhea for an average of one to two days and will require you to stay in your cabin with your roommate for a twenty-four-hour self-imposed quarantine—dancing all over every formerly delectable slice from here."

It was at that moment that Jamie and I wisely decided that we were not buffet people after all but dining room people, and this was confirmed with our first step into Château de Versailles, the ship's grand and mirrored cuisine hall, decorated exactly as if the specter of Marie Antoinette was expected to appear any minute in a cloud of ectoplasm and proclaim all of us "provincial" in a ghostly howl. I gawked in amazement as I walked down the steps into the hostess area that provided a full view of all the tables. Look at that, I thought to myself, no one's coughing or spraying saliva on a whole flock of baked chickens, no one's juggling three plates, each representing the cuisine from a different continent, and no one is already shoveling forkfuls of lasagna into their pie holes while waiting to scoop themselves up the fixin's of an entire meat-loaf supper and some chicken fingers.

Ah, the dining room, I comforted myself as I looked at Jamie with a smile in my eyes and nodded. This was where we belonged!

True, the selection of entrées wasn't as vast, but that hardly mattered when I realized that the lady at the next table had never had an opportunity to dribble her saliva all over my dinner before I did. We had our very own waiter who was only too eager to suggest which bottle of wine would best accompany our dinners and urged us to go on ahead and order a spectacularly crafted dessert. *The buffet?* Who were we kidding? This was a cruise, not a nonstop all-you-can-eat gorge at a Furr's Cafeteria! We loved the dining room so much it barely bothered us when the man who was seated one table over asked the waiter if the mango salad had meat in it, if the vegetable soup had meat in it, if the peach compote had meat in it and then went ahead and ordered a hamburger. His wife was also no day in the park; she wanted to know how everything "was prepared," and that included salad, soup, the main dish, and everything else she could possibly think of, including the ice, asking if it was "prepared with filter, mountain spring, or distilled water?"

After that question, the waiter stood there, silent for a good several seconds, deciding, I'm sure, whether he should deliver a nice, sharp slap to her with the laminated menu, bother to actually find out the origin of the water, or jump overboard and catch a cargo ship hauling very messy but very quiet wood chips back to his homeland of Croatia, where people were too busy trying to keep frostbite at bay to inquire about such ice-making nonsense.

Initially, I thought perhaps the wife's madness had a method, as in maybe she was kosher or a vegan, but it didn't. She was just an average run-of-the-mill pain in the ass who paid eight hundred dollars for an interior cabin with no window and then expected to be doted on simply because she was an asshole with an extra eight hundred bucks from her tax return who wanted to take a trip on the ocean but was too cheap to pay to *see* the ocean, just to get seasick from it. You know from the moment you spy the hordes of passengers in an enclosed space who has a window cabin and who doesn't. The people who dress identically in style and palette or in T-shirts from another vacation have a window. The people who didn't brush their hair this morning don't. The people who eat with utensils have a window. The people who subsist on a diet solely consisting of finger foods, mostly fried and of some variety of meat, and are more than adept at using a toothpick instead of a fork, don't. The people who encounter the man-sized dolphin character that stalks the ship both day and night in search of passenger prey and get a picture taken by his evil sidekick photographer for ten dollars have a window. The husband who stubbornly insists that his wife sidle up to the dolphin while the dolphin isn't looking and quickly snaps a frame, then proclaims, "I just saved ten dollars, Dolphin! What do you think about that? Watch out for that tuna net!" doesn't. They are the same people who would travel in the wheel well of a jetliner for a discount on the fare, then complain that the snack mix only had one almond in it. Damn right they're getting in the lifeboats last should it come down to that. And my neighbors the next table over were just of that ilk. That became all too evident when the waiter would explain a menu selection, as in, "It's chicken broth and vegetables," and she'd ask, "Is that French? Is that the French way to do it? I only want it if that's the way the French do it," or "Do you have anything with ginger in it? I am captivated by the taste of ginger. Ginger fascinates me."

By this time, I was almost hoping that we would actually strike an iceberg or at least a sharp rock, because the opportunity to puncture her life vest with a toothpick stained with barbecue sauce, accidentally knock her out of my lifeboat with an oar, or deny her access aboard my floating door was simply too delightful not to imagine. "No," I would say as I pushed her back into the frigid, inky water after she scrambled onto my float like a wet jackal. "This spot is saved for Jack Dawson, but I do believe I just saw a twisted, knotted ginger root float by that you could gnaw on until hypothermia sets in. Look on the bright side, though! You finally got to see the ocean!"

That fantasy went into four-wheel-drive mode when their dinners eventually arrived and I took a gander at her table manners, which included taking a long, overly involved sniff of every forkful before she dared put it in her puckery, picky mouth.

Another irregular, most likely windowless person I saw in the dining room was a man who carried a separate little satchel especially for the condiments he brought from home, including spices and exotic salts, all shelved seperately in secure little compartments within their condiment travel case. Not only did he have a wider variety of salad dressings than the chefs on the ship, he possessed every flavor of salad dressing known to Wishbone and Paul Newman, including a bottle of sesame ginger, which would have been enough to drive another windowless passenger on the ship simply wild with fascination.

Still, even with the sniffing episode, meat questions, and Purse of Flavors in the dining room, I was not even close to scurrying back to the Bacteria Buffet, where all the windowless finger-food passengers chowed down and spewed body fluids all over one another while wearing swimsuits and displaying copious amounts of body hair. There were, however, times when you could not escape the Buffeteria because you were sitting right next to them or telling them outwardly what cowards they were in several days' time (which honestly should have brought me dizzying joy in itself, but instead made me furious during my rampage as they continuously chewed on the pickings from the buffet that they'd rendered portable by wrapping them in paper napkins and stuffing them into purses or pockets, lest fifteen minutes pass without the opportunity to feed or consume something).

● ● ●

"**Didn't you hear** the man?" I found myself, days after our journey had begun, yelling to a group of buffet people as I stood on the banks of a glacial river near Juneau, dressed from head to toe in pliable yellow rubber like a weathered, salty old sea dog trying to hawk frozen fish sticks. "The guide just said that if we don't get one more volunteer to sit in the front row, we're not going on the river float! Now I don't want to be in the front row either, but my best friend volunteered, so I had to volunteer, and that means we need one more volunteer to equally distribute the weight in the raft, so someone in this group has to stop being afraid and lazy and raise a hand!"

Everyone had heard the guide, including me. That was precisely the problem. As soon as we were assigned a raft and had

gathered at the river, our guide informed us that it had been raining every day in Juneau for the past three weeks, and that meant
that the current was stronger than usual. Much stronger, he
added. Much, much stronger, he tacked on after the add. So
strong, in fact, that what was typically a nice, casual waft down the
river had now developed into Class III rapids, which, to an out-
doorsy, challenge-seeking person might seem like a piece of cake,
but to someone like me, who has an anxiety attack when a fat kid
cannonballs into a six-foot-deep pool, it could pose a possibility of
an issue. Plus Jamie had volunteered for the front row after our
guide made that disclosure and said that he needed volunteers for
the front because that was the especially wet part of the raft, then
stared at Jamie, saying nothing for an uncomfortably long period
of time until she relented and I was forced to follow. True, we
were the two youngest people in our group, but I had no idea that
kind of pressure was so effective on my best friend. Had I been
aware of this Achilles' heel, I would have been using it on her like
a swami during every lunch period in high school, saying, "I know
you love Wendy's, but we ate there yesterday and the day before
that and the day before that and the day before that. Today feels
like an Arby's day, and so does tomorrow, and the day after that,
and the day after that," and then looked her square in the eyes
until the spell was cast and I was scarfing on a Beef 'n Cheddar
and laying the foundation for getting my gall bladder ripped out
in twenty years.

"If no one else volunteers," the guide said after staring at
every other person to no avail, "we're just not going, and that
means no gourmet sausage and cheese snack at the end."

So, as a reward for our involuntary volunteerism, our guide

generously suited us up like greenhorns getting ready to wrangle crab pots in yellow slicker wear and life jackets so we wouldn't get *"very"* wet. By the time we got back to the bank of the river, a little middle-aged barrel of a man named Denny had been sacrificed by his beehived Texan wife, who was taking the last bite of a cheese danish when we arrived, to round out the front-row occupancy. He looked scared to death, and scrambled in between Jamie and me for the middle seat, stating that his chances of falling overboard were far less if he had a lady cushion on either side of him.

The guide instructed us to grip the wooden board we were sitting on with both our hands, with our "outside" hands at the end of the board and our "inside" hands between our legs, although with the amount of gear we were wearing and the mass of the slickers, I couldn't even reach the board with my "inside" hand. It's all right, I thought to myself, don't panic. It's not that big of a deal, he's an adventure guide, he's paid to make this little river-rafting excursion seem much more exciting than it is so we all think we're getting our money's worth. This isn't going to be any bigger of a deal than Splash Mountain, I tried to convince myself. Still, I looked over at Jamie and she looked over at me, not saying anything but letting me know she was scared shitless, too. Then the guide explained several times what we should do in case we got knocked out of the raft, and that we needed to try our best to get back in as quickly as possible because the water of the river had just melted off of the glacier and was only a couple of degrees above freezing.

Oh, sure, I thought, put on the big act. Get us all nice and frightened.

Then, with a push of the oar, we were away from the bank and floating down the river. Several other rafts filled with cruise passengers dotted the water ahead of us, bobbing along and drifting with the current. They didn't seem to be going too fast, I noted as I watched them for clues as to what was going to happen to our raft next. And then, *bink!*—just like that, I heard some short, pierced screams and one of the rafts was just gone as if it had simply slipped off the horizon.

I caught my breath and tightened my grip on the board with my outside hand. I held my breath and watched the water. It was getting foamy. It was getting fast. It was starting to rush.

I heard another cluster of screams, and I looked up just in time to see that the second raft had dropped off, too.

Then, right before me, the water began to swirl and dip, and suddenly it was far below us, as if we were perched high up in a cliff of water.

And then we began falling, and as everything in my body seemingly stopped—my heartbeat, my breathing, everything but my now electric sense of fear—I knew this had been a stupid, stupid mistake. *This is bad,* my instincts flashed at me, as if I could do anything about it, as if I could do anything but wait for one more fraction of a second before that gray, pearly, freezing water hit me. And in one enormous gulp it had me, it had us, it had the whole raft. As we plunged in headfirst—"we" meaning me, Jamie, and Denny—it smacked us with a wave of breath-sucking cold water that drenched us as if we weren't wearing any gear at all. When we emerged from the wave with a collective gasp, I was amazed that I was not in the water but still in the raft, clinging to the board as the current bounced us along and we headed toward another deep-water canyon ready to suck us in. Then I realized my new super-cute cat-eye glasses were not only wet but barely clinging to my head, and without thinking, I reached up with my inside hand and ripped them off, afraid of losing them in the next drop because there was no way insurance was going to cover something I had lost in the wilds of Alaska. But once I had them in my hand, I had nowhere to put them—I had no pockets in the slicker, and there was no time to undo the rubber jacket to get to my own sweater underneath. We were getting closer to the next set of rapids, and as the rushing of the water grew louder, I put my glasses in my mouth just as the raft turned diagonal and shot us down into another valley of turbulent water, and I hung on to the board as best I could, carrying my eyewear like a little dog would carry a stick.

I grunted as another wave swallowed us, and I grunted as the river tossed us all over, and I grunted some more as we fell into another dip. I couldn't do anything but squall like a terrified hominid as everyone else who possessed the gift of language beyond primal sounds screamed as the waves of the river hit us again and again. My mind raced. This wasn't the way this day was supposed to happen. We were supposed to float down the river, not tumble. I wanted to serenely glide past the scenery, not cling to a piece of plywood, grunting like a silverback with my glasses clenched between my teeth. As I was catching my breath but still too afraid to let go of the wood, we were finally pushed into a wider part of the river, which, though still swirling, was much calmer. The guide paddled us over toward a landing, where the two rafts I had watched disappear were already docked and were emptying of tourists.

My hands were frozen and still gripping the board when we docked, and I was finally able to look over at Jamie. She was drenched, with droplets of water clinging to her face. Denny, of course, was the first one out of the raft, and he leaped up and clambered over Jamie like a bow-legged squirrel, not even bothering to look back for his wife, whom I'm sure was probably too busy checking the dryness of whatever food supply she had tucked in her eighteen-hour bra anyway.

Jamie offered me her dripping wet hand and helped me out of the raft, and I followed her into the boathouse, where we removed our fisherman outfits and rubber boots, so traumatized we couldn't even say a word to each other. Under her yellow slicker and life jacket, Jamie looked like she had just stepped out of a pool entirely clothed. I looked like someone had dumped buckets of water over my head. Someone handed each of us a napkin with a loose assembly of a Hickory Farms summer sausage chunk, a slice of cheddar cheese, and a Ritz cracker. Someone else gave us paper cups with warm apple cider in them, which we gulped down.

That was enough warmth to enable my mouth to begin to form words again and release the frozen clench my jaw had been locked in to keep my glasses from flying out of my mouth when I was hit with the g-force of a river tsunami.

"That wasn't a serene float, that wasn't even Splash Mountain," I was finally able to say. "I feel like I just got waterboarded. I would have confessed to dating Carrot Top after one more wave!"

The sun was setting. We were freezing as we walked over to several large display boards with photos of people in rafts plastered all over them.

"Oh my god," Jamie finally said as she raised a soaked, puckery finger up to one of them in which a woman in the first row looked bravely ahead, her teeth clenched, her expression steadfast; the next person had his gray, middle-aged head barely peeking out of his raincoat like a turtle; and the next one, hair plastered to her head in a wet helmet, eyes wide and googly, fleshy face bisected horizontally by what looked like a twig, was about to encounter one of the many waves that was rising up to smack her in the face like a mother's impatient hand. Two additional outstanding features in this photo were the delight of the river guide, who was looking directly into the camera and grinning, and the possibility that a beehived someone in the last row appeared to be enjoying a bite of some sort of pastry.

"Oh, I get it," I sighed, looking up at a sign stating that each photo of us teetering on the brink of a watery death was ten bucks. "I need undeniable proof that we did this, otherwise people are going to say we got drunk and made the whole thing up. I'm going to get one, are you?"

Jamie nodded. "I'll put it in a frame next to my picture with Dolphin Man," she said as she took the final bite of her meager sausage slice. "But this is the last damn time I pick an activity based on the snacks."

To be honest, we were still feeling cheated about the lack of post-river-rafting/near-death selection of eatables, so as we were perusing the menu selection in the Italian restaurant on the ship that night, we decided it was only fair that we compensated ourselves for the ordeal. "I'm ordering everything I want," I announced to my friend. "I'm getting the chicken, the gnocchi, the salad, the cheese plate, the soup and I am asking for *two* desserts.

I am eating like a buffet person tonight! Don't try to stop me. You cannot. I have the appetite of a beast and the manners of a windowless passenger. I am insatiable."

"Why stop there?" Jamie said eagerly. "Let's get a pizza, too. And I'm going in for the antipasto cart. I want it all. *We are owed.*"

As we ordered, even our waiter seemed astounded at our degree of gluttony as we rattled off each selection and continued to elevate our debauchery with each additional demand.

"And bring us a bottle of wine!" Jamie said delightfully as she concluded.

But after the third course, we began to slow down, and when our second entrée arrived, we were nearing exhaustion.

"I never thought I'd say this," I said in wonderment to my best friend, "but I'm tired of chewing! My teeth are going to be so sore tomorrow. It's like they tried to jog."

"I know!" Jamie agreed. "How smart was it to order flan and mousse for dessert! All we have to do is swallow. Oh no! Don't look now, but here comes payback. I forgot all about the fifteen-cheese pizza with the meat-stuffed crust!"

We tried to act excited as the waiter brought it to our table and put a slice on each of our plates.

"That looks so good," I said, bravely trying to smile. "Look at all of that cheese. It's like a cheese blanket. There's enough cheese on that pizza to strangle someone. If you stretched all of that cheese out, I bet it would measure a length as long as my intestines."

"*Mangia,*" the waiter replied disgustedly and with a bit of a sneer before he turned and walked away.

We both stared at the slices before us as if they were roadkill and we were at the Clampetts' for dinner.

"Get this away from me," I finally said as I pulled my napkin off my lap and placed it over the pizza. "I can't stand to look at it. I wish we could give it to another table or abandon it at the buffet, where another family could take it as their own."

Suddenly, Jamie's eyes lit up.

"I have an idea," she whispered as she leaned in closer to me.

Fifteen minutes later, we were walking back to our cabin, the square box in Jamie's hands holding a three-pound meaty crust pizza within it.

"You are a genius," I said to Jamie as we both beamed, because there, at the end of the hall, were James and Ardhi, busy making their nighttime rounds.

"We've brought you something," Jamie said as we got closer to them, then handed them the box.

"Pizza?" James asked excitedly. "You brought us pizza?"

Jamie and I nodded.

"Thank you!" Ardhi added. "But we can't take it here, we'll get in trouble if anyone sees. Put it in your cabin and we'll eat it when we turn down your beds."

Remembering the image of sad James's and Ardhi's faces being left behind at the next port of call, I wasn't about to argue about their rights to hunger and sustenance, or the fact that when that layer of cheese began to solidify, it was going to take a blowtorch to get it pliable again. It frankly wasn't my problem. We had tried to do a nice thing, and I knew we should simply leave it at that.

So we went to our cabin and attempted to digest for a while until the boys showed up with big, wide smiles of anticipation. I didn't have the heart to tell them that the pizza had hardened like an old lava flow, but regardless, it was most likely better than anything they were going to get out of a vending machine down on their deck.

So Jamie and I left them to their pizza and wandered about on deck for a while until we passed the Sea-Saw Lounge.

"Maybe we should get a drink," I suggested, and Jamie was game, so we went in.

Suddenly, Jamie gasped when she saw an easel with a sign proclaiming that evening's entertainment.

"Can you believe it?" she cried. "Can you believe our luck?"

I shook my head and smiled. "A talent show!" I said, almost clapping my hands.

"Not just any talent show," Jamie added. "It's the *passenger* talent show! Oh, goody, goody, goody!"

We grabbed a table right near the stage and had been sitting there for approximately three seconds when a waiter asked for our order. It had been a rough day, we agreed, so maybe a twelve-dollar cocktail was in order, especially since the glasses were neon pink plastic and held about a liter. The waiter had taken only two steps away from our table when another waiter popped up and asked for our order, then another, and another. There was more staff in that bar than I had seen anywhere else on the ship, and their aggression rivaled that of the Dolphin Man and his camera pimp. I almost felt dirty; it was as if we had somehow entered a red-light district in Thailand and they were peddling virgins, attacking from every direction and trying to coerce every potential john with a cruise ID card to pick *their virgin*. And it didn't stop once our drinks came; in fact, one waitress told us to order several drinks at once to save on the time it would take her to walk back and forth to the bar. But at twelve dollars a piña colada, I wasn't about to waste my money. I didn't want to seem windowless, but I had approximately twenty thousand calories and four courses in my belly that my digestive system had to process and file before it could even begin attending to the alcohol, and to be honest, I've never let go of the college drunk in me. If I'm going to spend thirty-six bucks on booze, it had better be shooting out my nose by the night's end, and I'd better have some good bruises to show for it the next day, but at my age, when that happens you don't have a good story to tell the next day, you just end up sitting in a circle and spilling your guts to a collection of alcoholics (including at least one C-list celebrity) in a rehab center somewhere in Florida, so that's the end of that.

The talent show, however, was another matter. It was full steam ahead. Frankly, I think the world would be shocked to know just how many middle-aged, balding men would haul an electric guitar and an amp onto a cruise ship and stow it in a cabin the size of a McDonald's bathroom stall, because on our boat alone, there were four of them. This means that the number of Eddie Van Halens running around come Halloween are at epidemic proportions, and that sadly, an infinite amount of unrealized Angus Young fantasies are just waiting to spread their wings, shake out their ponytails, and fly aboard a Carnival cruise ship on talent night. Ain't we got fun.

Not that any of them had a chance of winning, not once *she* showed up, because as preposterous as it was to bring an ax and loudspeaker on vacation with you, it was even more insane to pack a pair of Rollerblades, a mini boombox, a flowing costume, and the recorded score for your "routine" and actually plan on using them.

I mean, honestly, I don't know where the Roller Queen imagined she was going to hone her craft, being that the walkways on the decks were more often than not merely several feet wide and all it would have taken would have been an errant crouton or a smear of butter to send those wheels flying overboard, past the balconies and Ardhi's and James's deck to the frothy surf below, only to become a small, forgettable segment on *48 Hours Mystery* about the looming dangers of cruising, inline skating, and wayward salad-bar fixings.

And that was too bad, too, because a little practice would have done her a world of good. The second the new-age harp and electric-piano music began, she was off to a strong start as she launched herself across the small stage in her chiffon and spandex ethereal finery, floating in an arabesque just like Michelle Kwan, except you would have to add three decades, 30 to 40 percent body fat, a divorce or two, a need for an extra-strength hair conditioner and a not-so-closeted gay boyfriend whom I suspect doubled as her costume designer and who snapped pictures from his seat on the other side of the stage. She completed the glide, and it was looking hopeful as she skated across the floor, waving her arms in the spirit of liturgical dance, all aflutter, and as the intensity of the routine music grew, it was obvious that she was going to make her first big move and astound us all. I couldn't wait. Then, in a maneuver worthy of a superhero, she threw both arms and one leg up as she caught air, her transparent fairy sleeves whipping around, and she spun, spun, spun in an axel jump and had almost rotated halfway until her orbit was grounded by gravity and the 40 percent body fat and she hit the hardwood floor of the stage with an echoing, resounding *thud*. She seemed stunned for a moment, and from several feet away her boyfriend/costume designer furrowed his brow and mouthed, "Get up! Get up!," his fists gripped tight, pounding against the air. She fumbled for a second, planted her hands on the floor, and raised her hind end, which was wrapped in a bounty of shiny black reflective spandex, made even more luminous by the rays of the spotlight that was directed at it and reflected off of it. It glowed like the moon—maybe even the sun—as she tried to get back up on her feet, but her tools of talent became her biggest obstacle. With every attempt, her feet shot out from beneath her like billiard balls, again and again, her ass raised high in the air, her shirt flipped over it onto her back, the moon glowing, glorious, and bouncing along the horizon with each attempt. Her boyfriend looked ready to burst into tears. But she didn't. Determined, she finally rolled around on the floor and then grabbed a column close by, and on the third or fourth try, was able to hoist herself up after being floor-bound for a good four and a half sips of my drink.

I was mesmerized, my eyes glued to her, unable to avert them for a second. She skated around the stage area again, waving her arms, extending them, flapping them like wings, running her fingers over her face. When she started gaining speed I knew she was going to go in again for another spin, and when she raised her arms for the jump, even I clenched my fists and furrowed my brow, entirely uncertain as to what I was hoping for. *Thud!* She spun out on the hardwood again, and this time she looked angry, as if the floor had reached up and grabbed her in mid-flight and pulled her back down to earth. This time she rolled over adeptly, grabbed the seat of an empty chair, and popped back up, and then skated around in a circle like a lost pigeon until the music stopped.

It was the best talent routine I had ever seen—part Isadora Duncan, part Jerry Lewis telethon—and I guess I would have felt some sympathy for her if she hadn't skated right back to the stage after the talent contest was over and she had bitterly lost to a red-haired lady who, it was obvious, owned a karaoke machine and a Mr. Microphone at home as she belted out an office-party-worthy version of "Cabaret." The Roller Queen picked up precisely where she last fell down, skating around and around as she forced her poor, supportive boyfriend to take picture after picture of her in defining poses, going back and checking the image for herself after each and every shot, for a good twenty minutes afterward, with no shame whatsoever. It was almost like an encore, and Jamie and I were so thrilled with the delights we had witnessed that we could barely walk back to the cabin we were laughing so hard.

"Spandex was a bad decision for her," I commented. "About as good an idea as mixing booze and tranquilizers."

It was when I opened the door that I immediately saw it sitting on the bed, looking up at me with little blue paper dots for eyes.

"Holy Christ," I said as I recoiled. "Is that what I think it is?"

"Oh, look," Jamie said. "That's so cute. Look! The boys made a walrus out of a towel for us!"

And yes, in a certain light, you could say that it might have been a walrus, as the towel was shaped in an arching upside-down

U shape, with its "tusks" represented by a bold swath that pro-
truded from the very center of the upside-down U. But in the
available light, I didn't see a walrus, per se. I saw a cookie, plain
and simple. Not the kind of cookie that comes out of the oven,
but the kind of cookie that falls out of your body and into the dirt
in Africa that you try to pick up with an even dirtier stick during a
stress-induced nightmare.

"That's a cookie," I informed Jamie.

"That is not a cookie," she replied. "It's a walrus."

"It's not a walrus, it's a cooter," I corrected her.

"You don't know what you're talking about," she replied.
"You're drunk."

"Hardly," I answered. "I had one drink."

"You had *four* drinks," she informed me. "You didn't even notice as they took away one piña colada and gave you another. You
just kept sipping."

"I'm drunk?" I asked. "Are you sure?"

"Yes," she answered with a definite nod. "I am drunk, too."

"That rocks," I decided. "Then I'm taking pictures of the
coochie."

Now, honestly, as I took photos of the terrycloth genitalia
from all sorts of angles and under different light sources, I wasn't
sure what sort of message Ardhi and James were trying to send
us. Was it to say, "Thank you for the pizza and we would like to
repay you in this manner, should you be interested," or was it to
say, "Have a good night you old lesbians, and here's a little something to get you started"?

I still haven't figured it out. But then again, I don't think it matters. They got a sort of semi-decent meal and I have forty pictures of a towel that remarkably resembles a giant walrus vagina.

"Will you stop that?" Jamie finally insisted as she took the camera out of my hand. "You've taken so many pictures already that you'd think it was Jenna Jameson on that bed."

"Shame on me," I said, shaking my head in disgust. "This is pathetic. I haven't been this drunk in years and all I can manage to do is take pictures of towel porn. God. What's happened to me? I haven't even fallen down yet or had my Drunken Meal of Frenzy. What time is it? Is it like four in the morning? Do you think there are Taco Bell tacos at the buffet? Hey! Let's go back to the lounge. Maybe if I trip a waitress we can get thrown out or I can provoke an angry verbal exchange with a Republican about foreign policy or funding for Head Start!"

Jamie sighed. "It's a quarter to ten," she said tiredly. "I'm taking an Advil and a Benadryl to fend off a hangover because we're getting up early to hike the Chilkoot Trail in Skagway. If you were wise, you would join me."

I gasped loudly. "What? And waste this buzz?" I replied. "Oh my god! Let's get this party started! I just remembered I have a Percocet floating around at the bottom of my purse from my last oral surgery. It's a little dirty, and it might be expired by now, but do you wanna split it?"

Jamie, who was already in her pajamas, gave me one last look and then turned out the light.

"Ow," I said as my shin smacked into the bed frame while I was trying to climb into bed. "I think that's gonna leave a bruise."

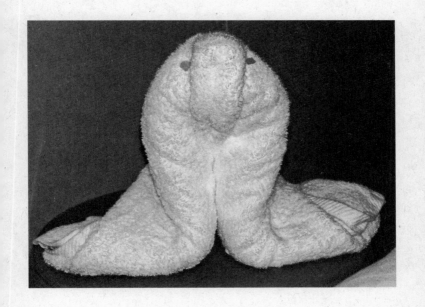

ACKNOWLEDGMENTS

I would like to extend my sincere thanks to the following people who were essential in the before, after, and during of the never-ending completion of this book, which took so long it has now become legend: the amazing Bruce Tracy, the lovely Jenny Bent, and the hilarious Lore Carillo (whose creative genuis gave birth to the ubiquitous "Flaming Tantrum" and whose generosity didn't permit her to argue when I announced I was stealing it), the guy who said it was okay to write that he touched poop in our basement, Libby McGuire, my family, Kim Hovey, Beth Pearson, Laura Goldin, Amelia Zalcman, Brian McLendon, Kate Blum, Diana Franco, Ryan Doherty, Dave Dunton, Jamie, Greg, Jeff Abbott, Dona Passannante, Meg Halverson, Bill Hummel, Kathy Cano-Murillo, Theresa Cano, Amy Silverman, Cindy Dach, Deborah Sussman Susser, Kartz Ucci, Erica Ashcroft, Heather Megyesi, Nancy Ragghianti, Grace Dunstan, Michelle Loyet, Michelle Jennings, Sharron Reed, and the rest of the cupcakes that I adore over at the IG board.

And thank you to my Nana, who I love and miss very, very much.

Muchas gracias,
Laurie

LAURIE NOTARO was born in Brooklyn, New York, and raised in Phoenix, Arizona. She packed her bags for Eugene, Oregon, once she realized that since she was past thirty, her mother could no longer report her as a teenage runaway. She is the author of *The Idiot Girls' Action-Adventure Club, Autobiography of a Fat Bride, I Love Everybody (and Other Atrocious Lies), We Thought You Would Be Prettier, An Idiot Girl's Christmas*, and the novel *There's a (Slight) Chance I Might Be Going to Hell*. She is currently at work on a plan B (to take effect when her book contract runs out) including selling hot dogs at Costco, selling hot dogs from a street cart, selling hot dogs at high school football games, or being the stop sign holder for road construction crews. At press time, she is still married, and she has an adorably disobedient dog that wears sweaters and loves chicken strips. (Clearly, Notaro has no children.)

ABOUT THE TYPE

This book was set in Caledonia, a typeface designed in 1939 by William Addison Dwiggins for the Mergan- thaler Linotype Company. Its name is the ancient Roman term for Scotland, because the face was in- tended to have a Scotch-Roman flavor. Caledonia is con- sidered to be a well-proportioned, businesslike face with little contrast between its thick and thin lines.